verbal
reasoning

course

Frances Down

DEDICATION

for Camilla, Clare and James
without whose patience and understanding of a mother
busy doing other things this book could not have been written

Published in 2002 by:
Nelson Thornes Ltd
Delta Place
27 Bath Road
CHELTENHAM
GL53 7TH
United Kingdom

08 / 10 9 8 7 6 5 4 3 2

A catalogue record for this book is available from the British Library

ISBN 978 0 7487 6724 3

Illustrations by David Mostyn
Page make-up by Viners Wood Associates

Printed in Croatia by Zrinski

CONTENTS

▶ Before you start

A very good question … we're glad you asked it. Verbal reasoning, or VR as we sometimes call it in this book, is a thinking technique … it's also an exam which you're probably preparing to take for secondary school … which we guess is why you've bought this book.

Verbal reasoning questions are basically word puzzles. They're designed to make you think and to test your reasoning skills … in fact they're intended to make your brain hurt. The aim of this book is to stop your head hurting quite so much – like aspirin really. Unlike aspirin it can also make a real difference to how you do in the exam. The people who set these tests probably think you should just turn up and do the paper – but we know that with a bit of careful preparation you can tackle the test more confidently – and improve your score. And that's what this book is all about. The secret is step-by-step practice – with the personal tutor to guide you.

HOW YOUR PERSONAL TUTOR WORKS

Personal Tutor consists of two bits. This book is the thing to learn with, and then there are sets of practice papers to use afterwards. This book teaches you all the skills. The papers then let you practise on realistic papers, similar to those you'll probably sit. You then go through your mistakes and learn from them. So, <u>use this book first</u>.

11+ personal TUTOR

verbal reasoning
course

- learn the secrets of verbal reasoning
- practise the skills step-by-step
- test and improve your scores
- your best chance at the 11+

FULL COLOUR

Frances Down

nelson thornes

11+ personal TUTOR

verbal reasoning
papers

- 4 authentic tests
- feedback to help you improve
- the best preparation for 11+

MULTIPLE CHOICE VERSION

Frances Down

nelson thornes

11+ personal TUTOR

verbal reasoning
papers

improve ...r 11+

Frances Down

nelson thornes

Your personal tutor guides you through all the skills of verbal reasoning in seven lessons. Here's how the course works ...

1 Your personal tutor takes you through every type of VR question, one at a time. These are in the yellow boxes.

> **1.1** | **Underline the two words which are the most opposite in meaning.**
>
> fox   day   vixen   river   night

2 It is then explained step by step exactly how to do the question. You'll always see the Personal Tutor showing you how to do it. You are given lots of handy tips and short cuts – and a few bad jokes as well ...

- Watch out for the catch here. Remember that it is <u>opposite</u> not <u>similar to</u>. It's amazing how often people get them confused! Fox and vixen are similar – they've been put here to confuse you.

- Work from left to right. First match fox with each word in turn to see if it fits:

  fox   day   vixen   river   night

Then day:

  fox   day   vixen   river   night

and so on... Even if you think you've got a good answer it's still best to check further on. Examiners are sneaky beasts... a pair of words may seem to be quite opposite, but are they the <u>most</u> opposite?

3 After every VR question type, you do a quick check exercise to make sure you've got the method. The answers are given upside down, underneath.

QUICK CHECK 2

> ▶ *Underline the two words that are most opposite in meaning.*
>
> **a)** (loud   expensive   gentle)   (dear   quiet   noise)
>
> **b)** (rear   fear   near)   (back   tear   far)
>
> **c)** (inside   insect   incapable)   (capable   side   sect)
>
> ▶ *Underline the two words that are most similar in meaning.*
>
> **d)** (splash   scrape   new)   (flash   flesh   fresh)
>
> **e)** (inside   extent   incense)   (outside   interior   outdoors)
>
> **f)** (thunder   snowstorm   hail)   (sleet   blizzard   lightning)
>
> SCORE   / 6

Quick check 2 answers: a) loud, quiet (watch out for similars!); b) near, far (confusing-sounding words, but meaning's clear); c) incapable, capable (focus on opposites and this is easy); d) new, fresh (be careful with similar-sounding words); e) inside, interior (watch out for opposites!); f) snowstorm, blizzard (the most similar)

4 When you get to the end of a lesson you get a 50-minute test paper. This practises all the question types to this point – as well as exam skills. The personal tutor gives you feedback in the answers at the back of the book. You can record your score by colouring in the chart on pages 94–95. If you have trouble with one particular type you are sent back to the tutorial again.

Test Paper 2

50 minutes

▶ *Put these words in alphabetical order:*

1 spin   span   spun   spare   spoon _____

---

5 The test papers practise all the skills up to that point – so by the end of the book you'll be practising all the questions from the lessons that might be set in a full 11+ paper.

6 When you get to the end of the last lesson you've done the whole course. It's then time to practise for the 11+ with our realistic practice 11+ papers. If you still have problems with any question types, the papers will direct you back to this book again.

DOING THE LESSONS

To use Personal Tutor you'll need:

* a quiet room ... can be tricky (especially if your sister's trying to watch TV in the same place!) – but important

* a sharp pencil (quite straightforward really ... if you have a pencil sharpener)

* a clock or watch when tackling the practice papers (the easiest thing of all)

* a fresh and uncluttered mind (no problem ...?!!!)

The lessons are complete units of work – but each one's longer than a school lesson. It's not really possible to do a lesson in one go. It's best to do a bit at a time. If you're doing this in the run in to the real exam we suggest that you could do a lesson a week – a seven-week course in all. Work through the lesson at your own speed. When you get to the Test Paper, stop – and do that another time.

DOING THE TEST PAPERS

The Test Papers are there to give you a realistic experience of doing a test under exam conditions. Each one is meant to be done in 50 minutes – and they get harder throughout the book, as new question types are learned in the lessons. Don't worry if at first you can't manage to do the whole thing in the time – that's part of what you're trying to learn in this book ... but there are some golden rules for tackling VR exams (and everything else in this book) ... and here they are – the Personal Tutor's megatips...

THE PERSONAL TUTOR'S MEGATIPS

1 Read each question carefully and at least twice.

2 When you tackle a question, always work from the left.

3 Write clearly. If you make a mistake, cross out the wrong answer and write it again clearly.

4 Keep an eye on the time – don't spend too long on any one question.

5 If you can't do a question quite quickly, put a mark by it and return to it at the end. Don't spend too long on any question.

When you have finished the test paper, turn to the answer section at the back and mark your work. Under the answers, there will be a brief explanation to help if you have gone wrong. If you don't understand where you slipped up refer back to the particular lesson and look at that section again. Use the flow chart on page 80 to help you analyse how you did. Work your way through that and follow any advice or instructions.

NOTES FOR PARENTS

- The lessons are designed to be cumulative and there is a progression in the test papers. Help your child as little or as much as s/he needs with the lessons.

- Please make the test papers at the end of the lessons as realistic as possible – so don't help with these. Your child needs to be as fresh as possible, have a sharp pencil and be timed for 50 minutes.

- It is important that your child learns from his/her mistakes and completes the follow-up work outlined at the start of the answer section to the test on page 79 to help eradicate future potential problems and to see where mistakes were made.

- Achievement in the tests also needs to be assessed in the light of how much of the paper was completed in the allotted time. As confidence and familiarity with the type grows, time should become less of an issue. It's important for your child to learn to use the time profitably and complete as much of the paper as possible to have the opportunity to gain more marks.

- Real VR exam questions are set in one of two formats – standard, where you write in the answer in an empty space, or multiple choice, where you are given a number of possible answers, from which you have to select one. For this reason the authentic sets of test papers which accompany this book offer a choice of the two formats: standard and multiple choice. Multiple choice questions always come with a separate answer booklet. All the questions in this book are in standard form – your child writes the answer in an empty space. The reason for choosing standard format here is that they're often harder. Multiple choice answer booklets can, at least, provide alternatives. Once the basic VR types become familiar, the technique of answering multiple choice can be quickly learned.

▶ Opposite and similar to

There are lots of VR questions about words which are the opposites of each other – day and night, black and white, heavy and light... and lots about words which basically have the <u>same</u> meaning... fast and quick, tiny and minute. It's important not to get the two ideas confused! There are several question types, some more obvious than others.

CHOOSING FROM LISTS ○ ○ ○

Here's the first typical opposite.

Megatip 1 – read the question carefully!

Megatip 2 – start at the left

> **1.1** **Underline the two words which are the most opposite in meaning.**
>
> fox   day   vixen   river   night

- Watch out for the catch here. Remember that it is <u>opposite</u> not <u>similar to</u>. It's amazing how often people get them confused! Fox and vixen are similar – they've been put here to confuse you.

- Work from left to right. First match fox with each word in turn to see if it fits:

fox   day   vixen   river   night

Then day:

fox   day   vixen   river   night

and so on... Even if you think you've got a good answer it's still best to check further on. Examiners are sneaky beasts... a pair of words may seem to be quite opposite, but are they the <u>most</u> opposite?

Answer: fox   <u>day</u>   vixen   river   <u>night</u>

Now here's the matching 'similar' question.

Megatip 1 – read the question carefully!

> **1.1** **Underline the two words which are the most similar in meaning.**
>
> fox   day   vixen   river   night

This time fox and vixen were the correct answer. It's essential to read the question carefully. Now it's your turn.

QUICK CHECK 1 ○ ○ ○

▶ *Underline the two words that are most opposite in meaning.*

a) dark	light	night	moon	star
b) shine	light	beam	fire	ice
c) fast	type	quick	kind	cruel

▶ *Underline the two words that are most similar in meaning.*

d) scarlet   azure   ochre   jade   crimson

e) juggler   burglar   logger   robber   angler

f) paste   piste   pasta   glue   flue

SCORE   / 6

Quick check 1 answers: a) dark, light (watch out for similars!); b) fire, ice (watch out for similars!); c) kind, cruel (watch out for similars!); d) scarlet, crimson (the only pair directly similar); e) burglar, robber (looks more confusing than it is); f) paste, glue (read the words carefully)

CHOOSING FROM GROUPS ◦ ◦ ◦

Here's a slightly harder type of opposite/similar. You have to choose a word from each group.

1.2

Underline the two words, one from each group, which are the most opposite in meaning.

(hour small huge)   (minute clock chair)

• **Start on the left and match the first word to each of the words on the right.**

(hour small huge)   (minute clock chair)

• **Then repeat for the other two words on the left. See which seems most opposite.**

• **This example again shows how important it is to read the question carefully.** Firstly, remember it's <u>opposites</u>; secondly, there are two meanings of minute (spelt the same but pronounced differently) – it's an examiner's trap! Minute can mean tiny or 60 seconds. Minute and hour are both units of time but they cannot be called opposites, whereas minute as in tiny is similar (careful!) to small – but the opposite of huge!

    Answer: (hour small <u>huge</u>)   (<u>minute</u> clock chair)

Here's the similar version.

1.2

Underline the two words which are closest in meaning, one from each bracket:

(perfect cradle moon)   (sunshine baby faultless)

Start matching left to right as before: perfect sunshine

    Answer: (<u>perfect</u> cradle moon)   (sunshine baby <u>faultless</u>)

The two pairs not underlined (cradle – baby, moon – sunshine) have some similarities or differences, but are not as similar as perfect and faultless. <u>Always look for the closest.</u>

Now it's your turn again.

QUICK CHECK 2

▷ Underline the two words that are most opposite in meaning.

a) (loud   expensive   gentle)   (dear   quiet   noise)

b) (rear   fear   near)   (back   tear   far)

c) (inside   insect   incapable)   (capable   side   sect)

▷ Underline the two words that are most similar in meaning.

d) (splash   scrape   new)   (flash   flesh   fresh)

e) (inside   extent   incense)   (outside   interior   outdoors)

f) (thunder   snowstorm   hail)   (sleet   blizzard   lightning)

SCORE   / 6

Quick check 2 answers: a) loud, quiet (watch out for similars!); b) near, far (watch out for confusing-sounding words, but meaning's clear); c) incapable, capable (focus on opposites and this is easy); d) new, fresh (be careful with similar-sounding words); e) inside, interior (watch out for opposites!); f) snowstorm, blizzard (the most similar)

CHOOSING FROM PAIRS • • •

This type of question is designed to make you think carefully … and to trick you. Here you've got to check pairs of words. (VR questions are full of 'red herrings'. 'What's a red herring?' you're probably asking. It's not a fish, but it is 'fishy'… it's a false clue put in to trick you.)

1.3	**Underline the pair of words most opposite in meaning.**
	day/night window/door cry/weep

Be careful you don't end up choosing similar words. And watch out – doors and windows are neither opposites nor similars.

Answer: day/night

Now here's the matching 'similar' question.

1.3	**Underline the pair of words most similar in meaning.**
	day/night window/door cry/weep

Remember to look for 'most similar'. Window and door are both to be found on a house but they could not be said to be either opposite or similar.

Answer: cry/weep

Now try your hand at similar and opposite pairs.

QUICK CHECK 3

▶ *Underline the pair of words most opposite in meaning.*

a) climb/trip   plain/pretty   split/spilt

b) whisper/shout   greeting/meeting   turn/curve

▶ *Underline the pair of words most similar in meaning.*

c) today/tomorrow   spare/sparing   creature/animal

d) glum/gloomy   plain/patterned   stripe/strip

SCORE / 4

RHYMING WORDS • • •

This is an opposite and similar question type which involves words that rhyme.

> **Megatip 1** – read the question megacarefully. Which word do you need to rhyme with?

| 1.4 | **Write a word that is opposite in meaning to the word in capital letters and rhymes with the word beside it.**
 BRIGHT bark _____ |

- There are two ways of doing this type of question. The simplest is to try words that rhyme with bark, until you come up with one that's also opposite to BRIGHT ... lark, park, shark and so on.

- You can work the other way – think of words that are the opposite of bright, until you come up with one that also rhymes with bark ... dull, dim, stupid etc. Quick fire trial and error is the answer – if one way does not succeed, try the other.

   Answer: dark

Here's the 'similar' version of the same problem.

| 1.4 | **Write a word that is similar in meaning to the word in capital letters and rhymes with the word beside it.**
 BRIGHT briny _____ |

- Step 1: Make sure you don't look for a word rhyming with BRIGHT ... what rhymes with briny?

- Step 2: If this doesn't work, think of words that are similar to bright.

   Answer: shiny

Now try for yourself.

QUICK CHECK 4

▶ *Write a word that is opposite in meaning to the word in capital letters and rhymes with the word beside it.*

a) FAST   go   _____

b) RICH   sure   _____

▶ *Write a word that is similar in meaning to the word in capital letters and rhymes with the word beside it.*

c) ASCEND   rhyme   _____

d) FLAVOUR   waist   _____

SCORE   / 4

Quick check 4 answers: (Always make sure you've found the opposite or similar!)
a) slow; b) poor; c) climb; d) taste

ODD ONE OUT

Sometimes similar and different questions ask you to find the odd ones out – the words that are different to the rest.

> **Megatip 2**
> – work from the left

1.5

Underline the two words which are the odd ones out in the following group.

colour red paint blue yellow

- These questions are often a lot easier than they look at first glance. Read the words through. Work from left to right.

- Try to group the different words: colour, red ... red is a colour; paint ... you get different colour paint; blue, yellow ... both are colours, so red, blue, yellow are together; paint and colour are the odd ones out.

QUICK CHECK 5

▶ *Underline the two words which are the odd ones out in each group.*

a)	spelling	alphabet	blackboard	desk	cupboard
b)	Lisbon	London	Libya	Lebanon	Las Vegas
c)	jumping	mumbling	hopping	muttering	climbing

SCORE   / 3

Quick check 5 answers: a) spelling, alphabet (the rest are classroom furniture);
b) Libya, Lebanon (these are countries, the others are cities);
c) mumbling, muttering (these are ways of speaking, the others are types of action)

WORDS IN HEADINGS ○ ○ ○

Sometimes you'll be asked to sort words into groups. It's another way of finding similars – but the good news is they're usually easier.

> **Write the similar words under the appropriate headings.**
>
> **1.6** zebra, gun, table, armadillo, armchair, dagger, jaguar, scimitar, gnu, cannon
>
> WEAPONS   WILD ANIMALS   FURNITURE

- This type of question is simpler than it looks and can be an easy way of gaining marks. It's often a matter of common sense. Even if you are stuck you should be able to make a good guess.

- Remember that the columns need not all have the same number of words. Sometimes a paper may even show you how many types there should be in each column by drawing lines for your answers!

Answer:	WEAPONS	WILD ANIMALS	FURNITURE
	gun	zebra	table
	dagger	armadillo	armchair
	scimitar	jaguar	
	cannon	gnu	

QUICK CHECK 6 ○ ○ ○

▶ *Write the similar words under the appropriate headings.*

a) cauliflower, garden, encyclopaedia, brewery, beetroot, churchyard, novel, diary, bean, dairy

PLACES	VEGETABLES	BOOKS
_____	_____	_____
_____	_____	_____
_____	_____	_____
_____	_____	_____

b) honeysuckle, oboe, orange, clarinet, ivory, tuba, tulip, claret, lupin, harpsichord, violin

COLOURS	FLOWERS	MUSICAL INSTRUMENTS
_____	_____	_____
_____	_____	_____
_____	_____	_____
_____	_____	_____

SCORE ____ / 2

Compound words

Enough of opposites – here's something completely different: compound words. 'What's a compound word?' you ask yourself. Simple. It's two or more words joined together to form a word which functions as a unit: honey and bee make a compound word honeybee. Back and bone make ...? Questions about compound words are usually of two main types.

MAKE A COMPOUND WORD · · ·

> **Megatip 2** – remember: left to right rules...a word from the 1st group comes 1st.

1.7

Underline the two words, one from each group, which when they are joined together make a compound word. A word from the first group always comes first.

(honey hare stone) (brush pin comb)

• Yes, it's dull – but always work from the left.

(hare honey stone)   (pin brush comb)

• Watch out for the spelling catches here. VR questions can be as slippery as snakes. Hairpin would be a compound word but not <u>harepin</u>! (A hare is the animal.) Hares don't have harebrushes either!

Answer: honeycomb

QUICK CHECK 7 · · ·

> Underline the two words, one from each group, which when they are joined together make a compound word.

a) (deck cup come)   (king board about)

b) (from with for)   (leg ever her)

c) (ring hoop tab)   (worm snake pole)

d) (shop shore shoe)   (sea sewing lace)

e) (smell shell shelf) (sting fish shrimp)

SCORE   / 5

Quick check 7 answers: a) cupboard (kingcup is a flower but here the words are reversed); b) forever (beware: there is a word foreleg but not forleg); c) ringworm (tadpole not tabpole); d) shoelace (not seashore because the words come in the reverse order); e) shellfish (mind your spelling – not shelffish!)

'ADD A WORD' COMPOUNDS · · ·

This is the second compound word type question ... and it's designed to hurt your brain – unfortunately!

1.8

Find one word which, when placed at the beginning or the end of the given words, makes a compound word.

BELL   GRASS   BERRY   PRINT

• These can be quite tricky. Usually the word to be added will come in front of all the words given – but not always. This has to be done through trial and error.

• Read through the words several times and experiment with different alternatives. Sometimes, if you don't see the answer straight away, it helps to look at the given words in a different order. (Yes I know we're breaking the left to right rule but sometimes ...) Remember that your answer has to fit all the words.

Answer: BLUEBELL   BLUEGRASS   BLUEBERRY   BLUEPRINT

QUICK CHECK 8

▶ *Find one word which, when placed at the beginning or the end of the given words, makes a compound word.*

a)	bow	forest	drop	coat
b)	light	burn	dial	set
c)	water	down	short	wind
d)	odd	foot	base	hand
e)	bolt	cloud	clap	storm

SCORE   / 5

Quick check 8 answers: a) rain; b) sun; c) fall; d) ball; e) thunder.

Phew, you've completed the first lesson. Close the book and have a break. When you're ready, try the test paper. It's best to do this on a separate occasion and to do the whole thing in one go. Take no more than 50 minutes – and look at the advice on pages 6–7 first. After that time, turn to the answers at the back on page 80 and mark your work. It's really important to go over your mistakes afterwards. Follow the instructions in the answer section on How did you do? Section on page 79. Remember you can always have another go at these questions.

Test Paper 1

50 minutes

▶ *Underline the two words, one from each group, which are the most opposite in meaning:*

1	(open ajar interior)	(closed inside room)
2	(off on in)	(off side edge)
3	(come three throw)	(arrive four catch)
4	(face false farce)	(fake genuine mask)
5	(many some one)	(time only few)
6	(gave given give)	(token take takes)
7	(expensive loved chick)	(dear cheap chicken)

7 MARKS   /7

1

▶ *Underline the pair of words most similar in meaning:*

8	sofa/table	bed/fridge	pillow/cushion
9	belt/boot	dagger/knife	lock/key
10	answer/explain	inquire/require	question/query
11	stormy/waves	calm/tranquil	thunder/lightning
12	sty/piggery	byre/barn	hut/house
13	pup/cub	sheep/goat	dog/hound
14	odd/even	level/even	morning/evening

7 MARKS   /7

▶ *Underline the two words which are the odd ones out in the following group:*

15	four	March	May	seventeen	sixty
16	dry	arid	parched	drink	throat
17	lizard	bear	crocodile	snake	dog
18	cry	moan	whimper	cheer	clap
19	right	wrong	left	incorrect	error
20	pool	puddle	lake	rushes	duck
21	yellow	green	mauve	purple	lilac

7 MARKS   /7

▶ *Write the similar words under the appropriate headings:*

22–33 bicycle   peg   wool   helicopter   cotton   tram
polyester   linen   basket   spoon   crayon   rayon

TRANSPORT   FABRICS   ITEMS

12 MARKS   /12

▶ *Underline the two words, one from each group, which, when they are joined together, make a compound word:*

34	(slight lamp lime)	(shade wood lamp)
35	(port part cart)	(stool wheel table)
36	(boy fellow man)	(cruel odd kind)
37	(ward word weird)	(rave ruin robe)
38	(hot dog fire)	(guard flame logs)
39	(fun won one)	(him self wealth)
40	(red reed read)	(book head bead)

7 MARKS   /7

▶ *Write a word that is opposite in meaning to the word in capital letters and rhymes with the word beside it:*

41	SHARP	grunt	_____
42	OLD	stung	_____
43	SMART	fluffy	_____
44	QUICK	woe	_____
45	WARM	rule	_____
46	HARD	croft	_____
47	HAPPY	glad	_____

7 MARKS   /7

▶ *Underline the two words, one from each group, which are most similar in meaning:*

48	(different similar odd)	(alike even quite)
49	(hot cold warm)	(taper tepid tapir)
50	(clever brilliant intelligent)	(slow sly shiny)
51	(pursue peruse perhaps)	(cheer cheese chase)
52	(steep rocky climb)	(ascend descend sloping)
53	(slip slide slither)	(mistake tread mud)
54	(rock cave rabbit)	(hair here hare)

7 MARKS   /7

▶ *Find one word which, when placed at the beginning or the end of the given words, makes a compound word:*

55	man	spawn	march	hopper	_____
56	colour	fall	melon	logged	_____
57	card	point	bulb	light	_____
58	black	spring	side	cup	_____
59	line	to	rush	going	_____
60	sky	star	night	fire	_____
61	one	how	where	thing	_____

7 MARKS   /7

TURN OVER ▶

▶ *Underline the two words that are most similar in meaning:*

62	birthday	presents	Easter	gifts	celebration
63	snow	ice	ocean	glacier	sea
64	sensible	endless	edible	senseless	reliable
65	creature	tree	plant	acorn	animal
66	fly	spin	twirl	dance	float
67	soar	linger	loiter	swipe	swoop
68	monarch	butterfly	rubber	ruler	net

7 MARKS   /7

▶ *Write a word that is similar in meaning to the word in capital letters and rhymes with the word beside it:*

69	EAGER	queen	_____
70	MELT	straw	_____
71	IDLE	crazy	_____
72	BEND	nerve	_____
73	SHINY	bossy	_____
74	STOP	fleece	_____
75	THIN	gender	_____

7 MARKS   /7

▶ *Underline the two words which are the most opposite in meaning:*

76	Friday	August	Summer	Winter	Tuesday
77	kind	caring	considerate	unkind	naughty
78	write	rite	sinister	right	wrong
79	gift	present	correct	abstract	absent
80	interim	interior	external	interval	exterior

5 MARKS   /5

TOTAL = 80 MARKS   **Now turn to the answers on pages 80–82.**

LESSON 2 ● Words, words!

► Words with two meanings

VR papers love asking you questions about words – for some reason. Worse still they love questions about words that can mean more than one thing. You can pound on the door with a pound – if you've got the money to spare … or catch a rash from a nettle if you're rash. You get the idea. The English language is rich in these types of words – and so are VR questions. Here's a typical VR question about words with two meanings.

2.1

> **Underline a word from the brackets that goes equally well with both pairs of words:**
>
> nurse, tend   pleasant surprise, gift   (present, care, treat)

- Take one word at a time <u>from the brackets</u> and try to match it back with each pair of words. Sorry, but if the answer words in brackets are on the right, then you'll have to break the habit of a lifetime and work from right to left – you can't always rely on examiners putting the words where you want:

  nurse, tend ✗ ←   pleasant surprise, gift ✔ ←   (present, care, treat)

- It's really important that you match the single words in the brackets against each pair of words, not the other way round – it's just easier this way.

- Usually each bracket word will go with only one pair. Only one bracket word will go with both: care goes with the first pair; present goes with the second pair; treat goes with both, as a verb in the first (you treat an illness) and a noun in the second (you get a treat for getting your VR questions right – perhaps!).

- Sometimes the answer will jump out at you. Other times you'll have to look a bit more carefully. Often you've just got to look at a word from more than one angle.

QUICK CHECK 1

► *Underline a word from the brackets that goes equally well with both pairs of words.*

a)	real, factual	firm, loyal	(true, trusty, devoted)
b)	savage, primitive	untamed, uncontrolled	(disorderly, wayward, wild)
c)	group, musicians	unite, join forces	(team up, band, bunch)
d)	tough, solid	difficult, complicated	(rigid, firm, hard)
e)	broom, besom	undergrowth, thicket	(shrubs, brush, dustpan)

SCORE   / 5

Quick check 1 answers: a) true; b) wild; c) band; d) hard; e) brush

19

WORDS IN WORDS . . .

Words are pesky creatures. Sometimes they hide other words. A wh<u>ale</u> can swallow ale for example, while a <u>beagle</u> can eat an <u>eagle</u>. (Because VR examiners wear anoraks they spend a lot of time thinking about this kind of thing. Then they ask questions about it.)

Megatip – the new word must finish the sentence to make sense

2.2

Find a three-letter word that can be added to the letters in capitals to make a larger word:

ST up straight and hold your head up. _____

• There's no one easy way to do these. Sometimes you get them straight away, sometimes you don't. Read the sentence carefully. Then experiment using the sense of the sentence to help you. <u>Remember the three-letter word can be added to ST in any position: before the two letters, between them or after them.</u> The chances are that ST will come together. Start experimenting:

STALK up straight and hold your head up. alk is not a word.
STARE up straight and hold your head up. are is a word –
but does the sentence make sense?

• If finding the sense doesn't work, try putting certain letters in. Here, if you think st is at the front, try a vowel: sta ... sti ... stu; or add an r and see if that helps: str

Answer: STAND up straight and hold your head up. AND is the missing word.

QUICK CHECK 2 . . .

▶ *Find a three-letter word that can be added to the letters in capitals to make a larger word:*

a) Please do not tread mud into the CAR. _____

b) I wish I liked STBERRIES. _____

c) At last, it is my T to have a go! _____

d) My COMER has crashed. _____

e) Help, the ship is slowly SING! _____

SCORE ___ / 5

Quick check 2 answers: a) pet; b) raw; c) urn; d) put; e) ink or kin

▶ Words hidden in sentences

When examiners get tired of hiding words in words, they hide them in sentences.

2.3

Underline the hidden four-letter word in the sentence at the end of one word and at the beginning of the next:

Look for the hidden word.

- These questions are (quite) easy – when you know how to do them. Here's how.

- Always work from left to right. (Sorry to have to keep saying this!) Look at the last three letters of the first word and the first letter of the second word. <u>Look</u> <u>for</u> ... ookf – not much of a word. Work along until you've been through all the overlaps between word one and word two: Lo<u>ok for</u> ... okfo, Loo<u>k for</u> ... kfor.

- Now go on to the second and third words and do the same thing again: Look <u>for the</u> ... fort – and there's your answer.

Answer: Look <u>for t</u>he hidden word.

QUICK CHECK 3

▸ *Underline the hidden four-letter word in the sentence at the end of one word and at the beginning of the next:*

a) Tie your shoelaces!

b) Look straight at the camera in the distance.

c) Off to market went the three little pigs.

d) Cinderella was made to polish and scrub.

e) She sang a calypso on the seashore.

SCORE   / 5

Quick check 3 answers: a) ours; b) rain; c) reel; d) hand; e) soon

Sorting words and numbers into order

Words and number sorting tasks crop up a lot ... all sorts of sorts really. You'll find that the question format can vary quite a bit, but don't be put off. The method is similar for all the examples below. Words can be put in alphabetical order ...

2.4

Put these words in alphabetical order:

saw   sit   sew   sow

_____

- These are easy if you know about alphabetical order. Start on the left and check the order of the first letters – they all begin with s. Look at the second letters: saw sew sit sow. A is the first letter of the alphabet, so saw is the first word and so on.

- Cross off the words as you select them and write them on the answer line.

Answer: saw   sew   sit   sow

- Of course you may have to sort by the third, fourth or fifth letter, but the principle is the same. For example:

stranger   straw   strawberry   strap

Words and numbers can also be ordered by size.

21

2.4

Put these words into size order, smallest first:

small   tiny   vast   large

_____

Smallest first, so tiny. Cross it off it and go on to the next in size: small and so on:

Answer: tiny   small   large   vast

> **Megatip 1**
> – read the question carefully

2.4

Put these numbers in size order, largest first:

15   1.5   150   0.15

_____

These ordering questions should be easy marks in a test but read the question carefully! Make sure you do as it asks – in this case the <u>largest</u> first: 150. Cross it off and continue. Thus:

Answer: 150   15   1.5   0.15

For some reason, VR tests also quite like asking you puzzles about people's ages.

2.4

Jane, Sarah and Sue are all seven. Jane's birthday is in March, Sarah's is in October, Sue's is in June. It is New Year's day today. Who is the youngest?

_____

The key here is the date today. You know all the children are 7, but your answer will vary according to when 'today' is. Here Sarah will have to wait the longest before she is 8 – she is the youngest.

QUICK CHECK 4

▸ _Put these words in alphabetical order:_

a) spend   spear   speak   scarf   stalk _____

▸ _Put these into size order, smallest first:_

b) 59   5.9   590   0.59 _____

c) mountain   molehill   hill   hillock _____

▸ _Put these in age order, starting with the youngest:_

d) butterfly   caterpillar   egg   pupa _____

▸ _These boys are all 12, but who is the youngest? It is November now.
Their birthday months are as follows:_

e) Bill January   Tom August   Sam March _____

SCORE   / 5

When you've had a rest from all this, do the 50 minute test paper. Then mark your work at the back, see how you did ... and go and watch TV, feed the hamster or annoy your brother.

Test Paper 2

50 minutes

▶ *Put these words in alphabetical order:*

1 spin   span   spun   spare   spoon _____

▶ *Put these in size order, largest first:*

2 hut   mansion   flat   house _____

▶ *Put these in order, warmest first:*

3 cold   tepid   colder   warm   coldest _____

▶ *List these in age order, oldest first:*

4 froglet   tadpole   spawn   frog _____

5 grandmother   great-grandmother   mother   grand-daughter   daughter

_____

▶ *Put these in size order, smallest first. Which is the middle one?*

6 0.71   71   710   7.1   7.01 _____ The middle one is _____

▶ *Put these in size order, smallest first. Which is the second smallest?*

7 0.7   0.005   13.3   0.09   1.6 _____ The second smallest is _____

▶ *By the end of the Christmas term, five boys in 5C were 11. Here are their birthdays: Paul: Nov. 2nd, Tom: Sept. 15th, Mark: Dec. 3rd, Hugh: Nov. 25th, Fred: Oct. 30th.*

8 Who was the last but one to have a birthday? _____

▶ *If these words were put in alphabetical order, which would be the middle one?*

9 pigeon   piglet   pigsty   pig   pigtail _____

▶ *If these words were put in alphabetical order, which would come second last?*

10 heaven   help   horrible   hippo   happy _____

(10 MARKS   /10)

TURN OVER ▶

▶ Underline the two words which are the odd ones out in the following group:

11	soccer	rugby	swimming	waterpolo	netball
12	tigress	doe	stallion	cockerel	ewe
13	square	cone	rectangle	cuboid	triangle
14	pilot	car	driver	train	aeroplane
15	Bristol	Wales	Edinburgh	England	Birmingham

5 MARKS   /5

▶ Underline the two words, one from each group, which when they are joined together make a compound word:

16	(butter	cheese	milk)	(mug	cup	stool)
17	(river	land	wood)	(point	blot	mark)
18	(cave	tip	pit)	(jump	tree	fall)
19	(house	ship	castle)	(wreck	ruin	rubble)
20	(eye	ear	mouth)	(sound	touch	sight)

5 MARKS   /5

▶ Find a three-letter word which can be added to the letters in capitals to make a larger word:

21 Climb up CFULLY. _____

22 At Christmas time we sing OLS. _____

23 My RAB likes carrots. _____

24 PIL fights are great fun. _____

25 What are you SPING you pocket money on? _____

26 How can you AGE those heavy bags? _____

27 The tramp SHIVE in the cold. _____

28 We have a choice of BY or soccer today. _____

29 The tiger SCCHED the tree with sharp claws. _____

30 He was NED from driving for two years. _____

10 MARKS   /10

▶ Find one word which, when placed at the beginning or the end of the given words, makes a compound word:

31	fast	neck	through	down
32	germ	grass	meal	ear
33	head	ridden	socks	spread
34	as	after	upon	by
35	port	craft	ship	tight

5 MARKS   /5

▶ *Write the similar words under the appropriate headings:*

36-45   salmon, dovecot, jet-ski, carp, stable, pike, minnow, bike shed, car, pram
FISH   BUILDINGS   TRANSPORT

▶ *Underline the hidden four-letter word in the sentence at the end of one word and at the beginning of the next:*

46   Robins lay three or four eggs.

47   Susie visits the shop every day.

48   I can't get the mouse on my computer to work.

49   She loved frosty winter mornings.

50   Some answers are more obvious than others.

51   They climbed slowly to the top.

52   Where are you going?

53   Please may I have that one?

54   Peter Piper picks hot chilli peppers.

55   In the shop we chose an assortment of chocolates.

▶ *Underline the two words, one from each group, which are most opposite in meaning:*

56   (red   yellow   white)   (blue   black   green)

57   (extra   special   more)   (even   peculiar   ordinary)

58   (fall   float   drift)   (swim   sink   scuttle)

59   (stairs   down   ground)   (climb   up   under)

60   (day   moon   star)   (light   beam   night)

▶ *Write a word that is opposite in meaning to the word in capital letters and rhymes with the word beside it:*

61   PLAY   lurk   _____

62   SLOW   aghast   _____

63   SOLID   follow   _____

64   CLOUDY   money   _____

65   FRAGRANT   winking   _____

▶ *Underline a word from the brackets that goes equally well with both pairs of words:*

66	begin, commence	jump, twitch	(embark, start, jerk)
67	attack, rush	cost, expense	(charge, storm, fee)
68	dirt, mess	earth, peat	(soil, garden, rubbish)
69	get on, climb	mountain, hill	(board, valley, mount)
70	herb, green	wise, intelligent	(plant, sage, shrewd)
71	unkind, miserly	average, middle	(median, nasty, mean)
72	place, point	pimple, blemish	(spot, position, bit)
73	considerate, generous	type, variety	(form, gentle, kind)
74	teach, coach	chain, series	(string, train, instruct)
75	fury, mood	lessen, moderate	(passion, modify, temper)

10 MARKS /10

▶ *Underline the two words that are most similar in meaning:*

76	slide	slope	skate	scrape	slate
77	skimmer	slimmer	shimmer	stammer	shine
78	clothes	peel	skin	foot	body
79	grizzly	clothed	hidden	bare	naked
80	excursion	trip	excavate	trap	extend

5 MARKS /5

TOTAL = 80 MARKS   **Now turn to the answers on pages 82–84.**

▶ ## Jumbled sentences

Jumbling up sentences is a common VR habit. They're a bit like scrambled eggs. It's all in there – but it doesn't look like the egg you started with. (Fortunately they're nearly always easier than sorting out a scrambled egg!)

3.1 | **Reorder this sentence to make sense.**
UNSCRAMBLE JUMBLED YOU CAN SENTENCE THIS?

- Start from the left – and read it carefully! (You're probably tired of being reminded by now!) Sometimes, by reading carefully, you can see the correct order immediately. If not, take it slowly.

- In this case it is a question, so it's likely that CAN YOU is at the start. Experiment, starting from the left: CAN YOU UNSCRAMBLE – so far so good. Continue along much the same lines, crossing off the words as you go. You should finish up with:

CAN YOU UNSCRAMBLE THIS JUMBLED SENTENCE?

The answer is YES!

Just so that you get the hang of it here's another example. This time only part of the sentence is jumbled. This makes your job easier.

3.1 | LAKE THE SWAM SWAN THE right across.
_____ right across _____

Here you don't have a question mark to give you a clue, so look for the subject, verb and object. The subject could be either LAKE or SWAN. Look at the verb – SWAM. Swans swim, not lakes, so swan is the subject. So: THE SWAN SWAM... Cross off the words as you go so that you can see clearly what is left and you will get:

THE SWAN SWAM right across THE LAKE.

QUICK CHECK 1

▶ *Unscramble these jumbled sentences:*

a) WITH TEA COME MAY I TO you tomorrow?
_____ you tomorrow?

b) LIGHT EVENING SUN THE THE IN glowed red.
_____ glowed red _____

c) PLEASE DOOR THE CLOSE quietly!

_____ quietly!

d) DANDELIONS, RABBIT carrots and grass EAT MY LIKES TO.

_____ carrots and grass.

SCORE / 4

▶ Suitable words and numbers

Here you have to choose appropriate words, or numbers, from a choice in brackets to make a sentence or sum make sense. VR papers love questions like these.

> **3.2**
>
> **Underline the most suitable word from each set of brackets so that the sentence makes sense:**
>
> I (packed, picked, poked) my (swimsuit, cabbage, larder) into my (hand, breadbin, suitcase).

- Remember your old friends Megatips 1 and 2. Sometimes the answer jumps out at you. Experiment with and build up the sentence slowly. Some alternatives can be rejected straight away, others you have to look at a little more closely.

- Work from left to right, matching the first word in the first bracket with those in the second in turn:

   I packed my (swimsuit, cabbage, larder) ... Say each of them in turn. Technically they all make sense.

- Try I picked my (swimsuit, cabbage, larder) ... swimsuit and cabbage are OK, larder isn't. Reject larder.

- Repeat with poked. None of them seem very good. Reject poked.

- Now go through again using the third bracket:

	(swimsuit)		(hand)
I packed my	(cabbage)	into my	(breadbin)
			(suitcase)

	(swimsuit)		(hand)
I picked my	(cabbage)	into my	(breadbin)
			(suitcase)

Choose the most appropriate.

Answer: I (<u>packed</u>, picked, poked) my (<u>swimsuit</u>, cabbage, larder) into my (hand, breadbin, <u>suitcase</u>).

The same procedure applies when dealing with numbers:

> **3.2**
>
> (9 16 25) ÷ (3 4 5) = (10 4 7)

- Use Megatips 1 and 2 ... careful question reading – and working left to right.

- Take the **9** first and work it through <u>all</u> the other brackets. You can't tell anything with number puzzles by doing only two brackets at a time.

$$9 \div \begin{matrix} 3 \\ 4 \\ 5 \end{matrix} = (10 \ 4 \ 7) \quad \text{No!}$$

- Now repeat for the **16**:

$$16 \div \begin{matrix} 3 \\ 4 \\ 5 \end{matrix} = (10 \ 4 \ 7) \quad \text{Yes!}$$

There is no need to go any further.

Answer: $16 \div 4 = 4$

QUICK CHECK 2

▶ *Underline the most suitable word, or number, from each set of brackets so that the sentence, or sum, makes sense:*

a) (12 13 14) (+ ÷ x) 7 = (3 19 15)

b) In October the (trees, leaves, squirrels) start to fall from the (leaves, conkers, trees) onto the (squirrels, conkers, ground).

c) Alex's (cat, hamster, dog) barked loudly when the (postman, cat, policeman) delivered the (letters, milk, newspapers).

d) "Why do you never (question, answer, sometimes) when I call (me, us, you)?" shouted (Mary, aloud, Wednesday).

e) (54 33 17) (x – +) (2 16 24) = 57

SCORE   / 5

▶ Matching words

These are quite straightforward to understand – but not always so easy to do!

3.3 **Choose the most suitable word from the brackets to go with the other two:**
leaf   petal   _____   (plant   tree   stem)

Look at the relationship between the two words on the left. Then look at those in the brackets. In this case, leaf and petal can both be found in plants and trees. Stem is the missing word because it is also part of either a plant or tree.

QUICK CHECK 3

▶ *Choose the most suitable word from the brackets to go with the other two:*

a) day   week   _____   (Wednesday   month   time)

b) feel   touch   _____   (ear   tongue   sense)

c) hat   beret   _____   (scarf   gloves   cap)

d) loch   reservoir   _____   (lake   river   stream)

e) gnaw   bite   _____   (tooth   bone   chew)

SCORE   / 5

Quick check 3 answers: a) month; b) sense; c) cap; d) lake; e) chew

▶ Word patterns

These are really just mini-crosswords without the clues. You'll find that they don't occur as frequently as other types of questions.

3.4   **Fill in the missing gaps with these words:**
SAD   TOY   DAY   SAT

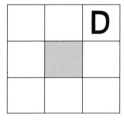

 • The clue should help you. Find a letter with a D at the end: SAD. Put it in.

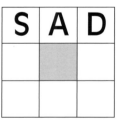

• Then it's quite easy to see where the rest go.

• Here's another version of the same thing.

**Megatip
– the letter clue
is your best friend**

3.4

Fill in the missing gaps with these words:

TIME   TILE   LAZY   EVERY   TOTAL

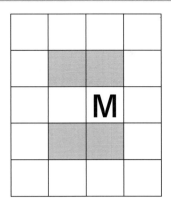

• A clue makes it easier. Find the four-letter word that has an M in it:
TIME. Put it in and the rest is simple!

T	I	L	E
O			V
T	I	M	E
A			R
L	A	Z	Y

QUICK CHECK 4

▶ *Fill in the missing gaps with these words:*

a)   FAT   RAY   TRY   FOR

b)   POET   ISLE   EAST   TREAT   PRIME

c)   REAL   OVER   TRAY   LORRY   ROOST

a)

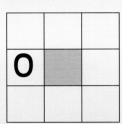

b)

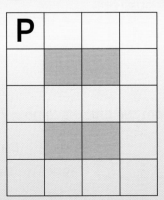

c)

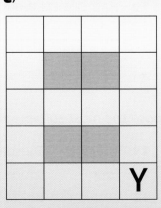

SCORE   / 3

When you've recovered from the excitement of this you can have a go at Test Paper 3. Then see how you did. Remember to go over the questions you found difficult again.

Test Paper 3 50 minutes

▶ *Unscramble these jumbled sentences:*

1 TIME IS WHAT SUPPER tonight?

_____ tonight?

2 SCAMPERED THE LITTLE THE THROUGH RABBIT long grass.

_____ long grass.

3 Pick up SENTENCE PEN YOUR THIS WRITE AND.

Pick up_____

4 THE SANK TRACE WITHOUT SHIP.

_____ (no clue)

5 She knocked ENTERED DOOR THE AT AND.

She knocked _____

6 PLAYED TOM PUDDLE MUDDY and I IN THE.

_____ and I _____

7 CABBAGE EAT ICE CREAM you may have an UP AND YOUR.

_____ you may have an _____

8 WAS KING TO THE SIGN JOHN FORCED Magna Carta.

_____ Magna Carta.

9 HELPING A SECOND I HAVE MAY please?

_____ please?

10 HAD SHE ELEPHANT AN WISHES SHE.

_____

10 MARKS   /10

▶ *Choose the most suitable word from the bracket to go with the other two:*

11 Thursday   Tuesday   _____   (Friday   March   Autumn)
12 fork   spoon   _____   (dagger   sword   knife)
13 cushion   bolster   _____   (pillow   sofa   bed)
14 robin   heron   _____   (lizard   owl   trout)
15 lifted   elevated   _____   (up   lowered   raised)
16 Atlantic   Arctic   _____   (America   ocean   Pacific)
17 noise   rumpus   _____   (hubbub   clang   whisper)

18	brackish	salty	_____	(sugary	saline	seaside)
19	wheat	barley	_____	(cereal	rye	bread)
20	bracelet	ring	_____	(necklace	bell	jewellery)

10 MARKS /10

▶ *Word patterns. Fill in the gaps with these words:*

21–24 DARE   CAVE   GANG   EAGLE   CAGED

	▓	▓	
	▓	▓	
		R	

25–26 NIP   TOP   BAT   BUN

	A	
	▓	

27–30 EDGE   SPAT   BOAR   TERSE   SABRE

	▓	▓	
	▓	▓	

10 MARKS /10

▶ *Write a word that is similar in meaning to the word in capitals and rhymes with the word beside it:*

31	FEED	wheat	_____
32	BROOK	shiver	_____
33	STREET	code	_____
34	TINY	cute	_____
35	LOCH	snake	_____

5 MARKS /5

▶ *Underline the most suitable word, or number, from each set of brackets so that the sentence, or sum, makes sense:*

36 Please (leave, arrive, come) to my (dustbin, party, elephant) on (teatime, Saturday, yesterday).

37 13 (− x +) (3 6 9) = (10 9 8)

38 James scored a (match, goal, season) in the first (match, goal, season) of the (match, goal, season).

39 (How, Who, Why) (is, are, was) (donkeys, butterflies, elephants) so brightly coloured?

40 (7 8 9) x (4 6 8) = (45 58 72)

41 (2 3 4) x (3 4 2) x (4 2 3) = 8

42 When mixed together, (red, blue, yellow) and (black, blue, white) make (clouds, green, grass).

43 Please (wipe, smear, paint) the mud off your (brushes, shoes, noses) on the (ceiling, doormat, radiator).

44 Simon has three (buckets, spoonfuls, cups) of (salt, pepper, sugar) in his (tea, supper, briefcase).

45 I saw a (camel, car, goldfish) speeding down the (motorway, classroom, river) being chased by the (tortoise, tree, police).

10 MARKS   /10

▶ *Underline a word from the brackets that goes equally well with both pairs of words:*

46 conclude, finish   edge, limit   (tip, end, close)

47 recline, rest   fib, falsehood   (untruth, lounge, lie)

48 declare, report   country, nation   (state, land, announce)

49 route, path   track, scent   (mark, smell, trail)

50 flimsy, unconvincing   disabled, limping   (lame, feeble, dull)

5 MARKS   /5

▶ *Find a three-letter word that can be added to the letters in capitals to make a larger word:*

51 My aunt grows lots of different PLS. _____

52 Do you like ILLA ice cream? _____

53 The children CPED their hands. _____

54 His KIT is fast asleep. _____

55 Please pass the TER and jam. _____

56 Sally has a BON in her hair. _____

57 Computers are GR fun! _____

58 Here's a birthday D! _____

59 TR live in clean rivers. _____

60 Too Y chocolates will make you sick. _____

10 MARKS   /10

▶ *Find one word which, when placed at the beginning or end of the given words, makes a compound word:*

61 side   shore   weed   _____

62 ship   field   ground   _____

63 straw   black   blue   _____

64 brain   song   watching   _____

65 side   light   work   _____

5 MARKS   /5

▶ *Underline the hidden four-letter word in the sentence at the end of one word and at the beginning of the next:*

66 Please attach your labels to your bag.

67 "Oranges and lemons!" sang the children.

68 Mum mows our lawn frequently in the summer.

69 When they went to Africa, they saw hippos in a river.

70 "It was all her idea!" complained Laura.

71 Having been shopping, my grandmother is now at the cinema.

72 Playfully he dropped two ice cubes down her dress.

73 Gemma skipped happily along a muddy path.

74 The boys tunnelled for hours into the sand.

75 On a searing hot day we drank nothing but ice cold water.

10 MARKS   /10

▶ *Put these words in alphabetical order:*

76 care   cast   case   cane   calm   _____

77 tang   take   task   tale   tarn   _____

▶ *Put these in order, largest first:*

78 11.4   114   0.114   1.14   _____

79 1kg.   1g.   100g.   100kg.   10g.   _____

▶ *Put these children in age order, youngest first.*

80 Amy is 3 years older than Chloe.

Lata is 6 years older than Chloe.

Lata is 1 year older than Sue.

Penny is older than all the others.

5 MARKS   /5

TOTAL = 80 MARKS   **Now turn to the answers on pages 84–85.**

LESSON 4 ● Letter change

▶ Completing words

VR papers are full of questions about missing letters. Enough missing letters to make a postman weep ...

FINISH THE WORDS ○ ○ ○

Megatip – it's got to be just <u>one</u> letter that fits both spaces.

4.1 | Write one letter in the space that completes the first word and begins the second word:

FIL __ ETTER

- • Look at each word individually. Say the first word in your head, and experiment with different letters. Repeat using the second word. Sometimes the answer is obvious.

- • If you have no luck, return to the first word. Go through the alphabet, letter by letter: FILA – no good, FILB – certainly not. Possibles would be: FILE, FILL, FILM, FILO.

- • Do the same with _ETTER using the possibles you have found. E, L, M, O – only L fits.

Answer: FIL L ETTER

QUICK CHECK 1 ○ ○ ○

▶ *Write the same letter in the spaces which will complete the first word and begin the second word:*

a) TAK __ ND

b) OVE __ OUND

c) SIMPL __ EAR

d) SPEC __ ING

e) SUR __ OAL

SCORE / 5

Quick check 1 answers: a) E; b) R; c) Y; d) K; e) F

FINISH THE WORD PAIRS ○ ○ ○

This time you have to find one letter to finish two pairs of words. The method is exactly the same as the last one, but the question wording is different and you are given an extra clue to the answer – which actually makes it easier.

4.2 | Find one letter that will complete both sets of words:

STA __ EAR   PLA __ OUR

- Work through the alphabet, checking letters that fit the first set. Answers could be: STAB BEAR, STAG GEAR, STAR REAR, STAY YEAR.

- Now see which of these answer letters fit the second pair: B, G, R, Y. The only possibility for the second pair is: PLAY YOUR, so the answer is:
STAY   YEAR   PLAY   YOUR

QUICK CHECK 2

▶ *Find one letter that will complete both sets of words:*

a) EAC __ ALL   WIT __ EEL

b) SIN __ REY   DUN __ LUM

c) MAN __ ASY   FRE __ NVY

d) REA __ EAR   WAR __ ELT

e) SAL __ ALL   WAI __ ILE

SCORE ___ / 5

Quick check 2 answers: a) H; b) G; c) E; d) P; e) T

▶ Anagrams

Anagrams are words that have had their eltrtes jumbled up, so to speak. There are several varieties of anagrams that appear in **VR** tests. These are the common ones.

DEFINITION CLUES ○ ○ ○

Some are placed in sentences that give a definition to help you.

4.3 | **Arrange the letters in capitals into a word that makes sense in the sentence.**
A RDISPE spins a web and has eight legs.

- Of course this one's a doddle. The clue tells you straightaway that it's a spider. Unfortunately in exams they're not always so easy. Always start by using your best clue – the meaning of the sentence.

- If this still doesn't work you'll have to start rearranging individual letters. Look at the number of vowels and place the consonant blends together. RDISPE only has two vowels, so there must be at least one consonant blend: DR, PR, SP. Practise fitting in the other letters using these blends at the beginning: DRISPE – not a word, PRISED – a word, but does it make sense? – no, SPIDER – success!

QUICK CHECK 3

▶ *Work out these anagrams and write the correct word on the line:*

a) Matthew drew the bedroom STRAINUC before he went to bed. _____

b) A STEMICH dispenses medicines to people. _____

c) Julie put her bag on her desk and took out her WROMEOKH. _____

d) A YMAPALET is a friend with whom a child plays. _____

e) The stars seemed very THGRBI in the moonlit sky. _____

SCORE   / 5

Quick check 3 answers: a) curtains; b) chemist; c) homework; d) playmate; e) bright

WORDS WITHIN WORDS ○ ○ ○

Anagrams can also take the form of smaller words within longer ones.
VR exam setters love this kind of thing. This may involve looking
for the odd one out. Here are two types.

Megatip 1
– read the questions
even more carefully

4.4

**Underline the word from the list that cannot be made
using the letters from the long word:**

REASONING   noise   sonar   raising   snore

**Underline the word from the list that can be made
using the letters from the long word:**

REASONING   snores   grease   raining   region

- We never tire of saying this but ... <u>always start on the left</u>, except when
  you are told not to. Work through methodically, checking the letters in
  the words on the right one by one against the word in capitals. Cross the
  letters in the smaller words off as you find them. Don't mark your source
  word REASONING, otherwise you'll quickly confuse yourself.

- <u>Remember that each letter can only be used once.</u> Here there are
  two N's, so you may use them twice. So in raining the two N's are
  all right but not the two I's – there's only one I in REASONING.
  The answers are:

  REASONING   noise   sonar   <u>raising</u>   snore

  REASONING   snores   grease   raining   <u>region</u>

QUICK CHECK 4 ○ ○ ○ ○

Underline the word that cannot be made from the long word:

a) PRESSURE   press   rush   peers   pure

b) CROSSING   scorn   rings   gross   cringe

c) POSTMAN   maps   most   pants   stunt

Underline the word that can be made from the long word:

d) SPLENDID   spied   nested   landed   diner

e) CAPITAL   plate   tapioca   tail   palace

f) TERRIBLE   bride   bleat   river   tribe

SCORE   / 6

38

Quick check 4 answers: a) rush; b) cringe; c) stunt; d) spied; e) tail; f) tribe

SAME LETTERED WORDS ○ ○ ○

Here you have to look for the pair of anagrams.

4.5 **Underline the two words that are made from the same letters:**
story   steal   yeast   least   years   trees

Start on the left! Compare the letters in story with each successive word:

story   steal   yeast   least   years   trees

story and steal? No. story and yeast? No. story and least? No.
story and years? No. story and trees? No. Start again with steal:

story   steal   yeast   least   years   trees

If you keep going, you'll get to the answer in the end, which is:

story   <u>steal</u>   yeast   <u>least</u>   years   trees

QUICK CHECK 5 ○ ○ ○

Underline the two words that are made from the same letters:

a) train   stair   steer   trees   rails
b) loser   roses   rails   soils   sores
c) plane   panel   lapel   plain   nails
d) start   treat   taste   tarts   steer
e) steel   pleat   table   spate   sleet

SCORE   / 5

Quick check 5 answers: a) steer trees; b) roses sores; c) plane panel; d) start tarts; e) steel sleet

Have a breather, have a rest, do your paper round or whatever, then come back to Test Paper 4 another time.

Test Paper 4

5○ minutes

Underline the word that can be made from the long word:

1 FAVOURITE   trivia   forty   rift   trout
2 PRECIOUS   scope   races   used   cross
3 CYLINDER   lender   cinder   rinse   linger
4 SCORPION   score   prince   croon   opinion
5 TENUOUS   sonnet   stun   noses   nests

5 MARKS   /5

4

▶ *Work out these anagrams and write the correct word on the line:*

6 A FRAGIFE is an animal with a long neck. _____

7 Your torch is powered by one large TRYBATE. _____

8 Many KNESA venoms are highly poisonous. _____

9 A group of five people is called a NUTTEIQ. _____

10 My grandfather has a TRIPCUE of the Queen on his wall. _____

11 To be ELIBOM means to be able to move about freely. _____

12 Snakes and DRELDAS is my little brother's favourite game. _____

13 A BAMISRUEN is a warship that is able to be completely submerged in the sea for long periods of time. _____

14 Please settle down to your homework TILEYUQ. _____

15 To ZUGZEL is to eat or drink greedily. _____

10 MARKS /10

▶ *Write the same letter in the space to complete the first word and begin the second word:*

16 PAG __ VEN

17 HOO __ ILM

18 PIN __ HIS

19 TRI __ INK

20 SPO __ WIN

21 GON __ APE

22 ARE __ LSO

23 TEA __ OTA

24 EAT __ EAT

25 PLA __ OSE

10 MARKS /10

▶ *Choose the most suitable word from the brackets to go with the other two:*

26 pit   colliery   (mine   yours   hers)

27 puppy   calf   (dog   cow   kitten)

28 restore   repair   (repay   fix   install)

29 alike   related   (cousin   similar   compare)

30 erect   vertical   (steep   downright   upright)

5 MARKS /5

▶ *Underline the two words that are made from the same letters:*

31 zonal   lazes   snail   slope   poles

32 crane   march   scram   cream   charm

33 plate   table   bleat   staple   please

34	laser	nasal	slain	pines	snipe
35	grape	great	pager	greet	tripe
36	bushy	shunt	brush	scrub	shrub
37	moons	limes	storm	smile	spoon
38	clasp	scalp	paste	spite	price
39	strip	slate	first	stiff	stale
40	beers	tribe	bards	beard	bread

⊸——————————————————————————————————⟨ 10 MARKS   /10 ⟩

▶ *Find a four-letter word that can be added to the letters in capitals to make a larger word:*

41 On cold mornings it can be difficult to S the car. _____

42 Please calm down and be REASON. _____

43 He CED up the tree swiftly. _____

44 The judge ENCED the thief to five years in prison. _____

45 The black HER crept along the branch unseen by its prey. _____

⊸——————————————————————————————————⟨ 5 MARKS   /5 ⟩

▶ *Fill in the missing gaps with these words:*

46–47 pan   pip   tan   pat

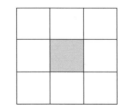

48–51 sight   glade   sing   gala   tote

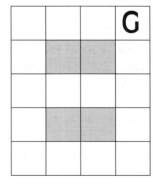

52–55 every   flame   acre   envy   fire

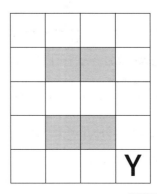

⊸——————————————————————————————————⟨ 10 MARKS   /10 ⟩

TURN OVER ▶

▶ Underline the word that cannot be made from the long word:

56	PLEASANT	plea	sane	apple	nasal
57	TRANSPARENT	parent	entrap	nearest	spartan
58	BREAKFAST	stack	feast	streak	fakes
59	TREASURE	sure	trust	rates	steer
60	FLAVOURING	fling	groin	valour	saviour

5 MARKS /5

▶ Find one letter that will complete and start each set of words:

61	PON __ OUR	PLA __ ARD
62	MIL __ EPT	TAL __ ITE
63	CAL __ ROM	REE __ LAT
64	LIM __ ARL	TAL __ ASY
65	SOF __ CRE	FLE __ BLE
66	PLU __ INK	CLA __ EAT
67	FIS __ IDE	BAT __ EAL
68	GEA __ AID	STI __ ATE
69	STO __ EAR	FLA __ ALK
70	WOR __ OOR	SLI __ ORE

10 MARKS /10

▶ Underline the two words, one from each group, which are most similar in meaning:

71	(suet	pudding	oasis)	(sweat	desert	dessert)
72	(pin	pen	pan)	(sauce	pot	sharp)
73	(mix	corn	combine)	(harvester	join	field)
74	(always	towards	too)	(and	alas	also)
75	(drizzle	splash	drop)	(crash	rain	grey)

5 MARKS /5

▶ Underline the hidden four-lettered word in the sentence at the end of one word and at the beginning of the next:

76 Our cat wins prizes at the show for pedigree cats.

77 He doesn't have much in his money box.

78 Shall I wear my pink and yellow pyjamas?

79 The camel ambled towards the watering hole.

80 He was wearing a blue jacket and a mauve ill-fitting shirt.

5 MARKS /5

TOTAL = 80 MARKS   Now turn to the answers on pages 85–87.

▶ Moving letters

When letters aren't missing in **VR** papers, they're on the move … restless little creatures really! There are several different question types in which words are changed letter by letter to make new words.

Megatip – you're only adding <u>one</u> letter

5.1 **Make a new word by adding a letter using the written clue:**

word _____ (a weapon with a sharp blade)

• Your best method is using the clue. Look at it carefully – it's your friend. Remember that the word is only changing by one letter. If you still can't see the answer, experiment with putting in different letters – at the start, end or middle of the word.

Answer: word   sword (a weapon with a sharp blade)

• Here's another one to sharpen your sword skills on, so to speak. The missing letter's not at the start this time.

5.1 nice _____ (your sister's daughter)

The clue here will probably be sufficient. If not, you know the word begins with n, so split nice into parts and see where you can put another letter in.

Answer: nice   niece (your sister's daughter)

QUICK CHECK 1

▶ *Make a new word by adding a letter using the written clue:*

a) late _____ (your meal is served on one)

b) crow _____ (a king wears one)

c) bride _____ (a horse wears one)

d) sting _____ (thin rope)

e) prates _____ (they rob ships)

SCORE   / 5

Quick check 1 answers: a) plate; b) crown; c) bridle; d) string; e) pirates

43

REMOVE A LETTER ...

5.2 | **Make a new word by taking away a letter using the written clue:**

sword _____ (made up of letters)

This type is the exact opposite of the one before. Approach it in the same way, except remember to take a letter away. It is much easier to experiment because the letters are already there. Try crossing out each letter in turn if you like. Start at the left: ʂword ... you've got the answer straight away!

Answer: sword   word   (made up of letters)

QUICK CHECK 2

▶ *Make a new word by taking away a letter using the written clue:*

a) pray _____ (a shaft of light)

b) flick _____ (use your tongue)

c) spine _____ (twirl)

d) plain _____ (an ache)

e) flay _____ (an insect)

SCORE / 5

Quick check 2 answers: a) ray; b) lick; c) spin; d) pain; e) fly

ONE LETTER, MANY WORDS ...

Here you have to add just one letter to lots of words.

5.3 | **Find one letter that goes in front of all the given words to make new words:**

_word   _nail   _low   _way

Trial and error is the best way here. You can just work through the alphabet if you like: a, b, c and so on. Start on the left as always.

Answer: ʂword   ʂnail   ʂlow   ʂway

QUICK CHECK 3

▶ *Find one letter that goes in front of all the given words to make new words:*

a) __row   __art   __love

b) __here   __rain   __angle

c) __lame   __risky   __ore

d) __way   __bound   __loft

e) __love   __rim   __host

SCORE / 5

CHANGING LETTERS ○ ○ ○

Here you change a word, step by step, one letter at a time, into another word. For example rat, rag, rug. These can be quite tricky.

5.4	**Change the first word into the last word by changing one letter at a time and making a new word in the middle.**
	KNEW _ _ _ _ KNOT

- Step 1: With your pencil, underline the letters in <u>KN</u>OT that are the same as the original word <u>KN</u>EW: KN. Write these in the same place in the mystery word:

- <u>KN</u>EW   K N _ _   <u>KN</u>OT

- Step 2: the mystery word can only be one letter different from both KNEW and KNOT. Look at the letters which are different between KNOT and KNEW: OT and EW. Either the W must change to T:

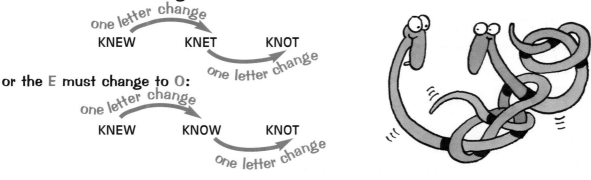

one letter change

KNEW   KNET   KNOT

one letter change

or the E must change to O:

one letter change

KNEW   KNOW   KNOT

one letter change

The answer must be a real word, so it's KNOW. This provides the step between KNEW and KNOT.

Do these the same way.

QUICK CHECK 4 ○-○-○

▶ *Change the first word into the last word by changing one letter:*

a) PRAM _ _ _ _ FRAY

b) LIMB _ _ _ _ TIME

c) NAIL _ _ _ _ TOIL

d) FLAT _ _ _ _ NEAT

e) TAME _ _ _ _ SANE

SCORE / 5

TWO STEP CHANGES · · ∘

This is the same idea, only you need two steps from the first to the last word – they're a bit harder still!

5.5 | **Change one letter at a time to create two new words in the middle.**

CART _ _ _ _   _ _ _ _ BATE

- Follow exactly the same method as before. You just need to take a little more care.

- Step 1: Find and write in any letter that remains the same all the time: A.

CART _A _ _   _A _ _ BATE

- Step 2: What <u>one</u> letter could you change in CART, and still make a word? <u>It will be one of the other letters in the word at the end: BATE: B, T or E</u>. Try:

   B?   T?   E?

CART – BART – not a word ... CATT – no ... CARE ... yes a word. Write it in. So you now have:

CART   CARE   _ A _ E   BATE

- Step 3: Now you're looking to change one letter in CARE and still make a word. It will be one of the other letters in BATE: B or T. Try:

   B? T?

CARE – BARE ... yes a word. CATE ... not a word. So the full answer is:

CART   CARE   BARE   BATE

Simple really! Now try these yourself. Follow the step-by-step method.

QUICK CHECK 5 · ∘ ∘

a)	BORN	_ _ _ _	_ _ _ _	SOME
b)	PICK	_ _ _ _	_ _ _ _	MACE
c)	DISH	_ _ _ _	_ _ _ _	RASP
d)	SWAN	_ _ _ _	_ _ _ _	SKIM
e)	HILL	_ _ _ _	_ _ _ _	PINE

SCORE   / 5

LEND A LETTER · ∘ ∘

5.6 | **Move one letter from the first word to the second word to give two new words:**

STOP   LOW _ _ _ _ _ _   _ _ _ _ _ _

• These are quite easy. You know you've got to take a letter from the first word. Which letter could be moved from it <u>so that the remaining letters still make a word on their own?</u> TOP or SOP would still both be words if you take out S or T.

• Now try adding the S or the T to the second word. Try fitting the S into LOW... SLOW is a word. Check T with LOW. No good.

Answer: STOP   LOW   TOP   SLOW

Now try these.

QUICK CHECK 6

a)	CRAM	LAP	_____	_____
b)	BITE	MAN	_____	_____
c)	ROPE	EAR	_____	_____
d)	STEW	ONE	_____	_____
e)	PILE	TOO	_____	_____

SCORE   / 5

Quick check 6 answers: a) RAM CLAP; b) BIT MANE; c) ROE PEAR; d) SEW TONE; e) PIE TOOL

MAKE A PAIR ○ ○ ○

Here you have to use a pattern in a pair of words to complete a second pair.

5.7   **Write the missing word of the second pair of words in the same way as the first pair has been made:**
rang   bang   rung   _____

You need to check two things here. Firstly, look at the relationship of rang and bang – they rhyme. Secondly, look at the relationship of the <u>first words in both pairs</u>, rang and rung. What's happened? Easy, ang has become ung. Now change the second word of the first pairing, bang, the same way as rang has been treated.

Answer: rang   bang   rung   <u>bung</u>

Now try these.

QUICK CHECK 7 ○—○

a)	barn	tarn	born	_____
b)	stern	still	tern	_____
c)	grime	prime	grim	_____

d) split   strew   spit   _____

e) blue   clue   flue   _____

SCORE   / 5

Quick check 7 answers: a) torn; b) till; c) prim; d) stew (the third letters in split and strew have been taken away); e) glue (letter substitution by the next letter in the alphabet has taken place in this group)

FOLLOW A PATTERN ○ ○ ○

Warning: this particular little group can be brain benders – but if you follow the method below step by step you can see how to do it!

> **5.8**   **Find the missing word in the second group by following the same series of steps that created the underlined word in the first group:**
>   PREY   <u>PRAM</u>   MAIN   STEW   _ _ _ _   YARD

- The second set of words follows exactly the same set of steps as the first one. You do this by working out how the word in the middle PRAM was made from the two words either side – and then using the same rules in the second group. The trick is to see exactly where the letters in the middle word have come from. Study this very carefully!

These go here ➝   ↖ These went here – but they were turned round

| P R | E Y | | P R | A M | | M A | I N |

- Now you use the same pattern with the second set:

These go here ➝   ↖ These go here – but you must turn them round

| S T | E W | | _ _ | _ _ | | Y A | R D |

so the answer is STAY

Easy? Let's do another one – and let's make it just a little harder!

> **5.8**   **Find the missing word in the second group by following the same series of steps that created the underlined word in the first group:**
>   FILE   <u>LEFT</u>   TENS   PIGS   _ _ _ _   EACH

- Get your microscope out in the same way. You quickly see a problem. It could be:

| F | I | L | E | | L | E | F | T | | T | E | N S |

or it could be:

| F | I | L | E | | L | E | F | T | | T | E | N S |

the pesky E could come from FILE or TENS!

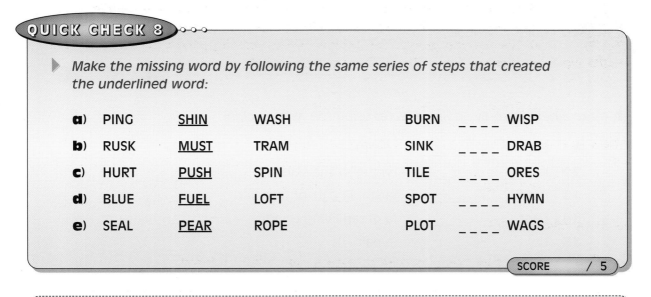

• So you'll have to try out both possibilities on the second pair. Here goes …

Try this pattern: F I L E   L E F T   T E N S

You get: P I G S   G S P E   E A C H

GSPE? It may mean something in Martian – but let's try again.

Now try this one: F I L E   L E F T   T E N S

You get: P I G S   G A P E   E A C H

GAPE? That looks like a real word … hurrah!

Now you try these – and good luck!

QUICK CHECK 8

▶ *Make the missing word by following the same series of steps that created
the underlined word:*

a)	PING	<u>SHIN</u>	WASH	BURN	_ _ _ _	WISP
b)	RUSK	<u>MUST</u>	TRAM	SINK	_ _ _ _	DRAB
c)	HURT	<u>PUSH</u>	SPIN	TILE	_ _ _ _	ORES
d)	BLUE	<u>FUEL</u>	LOFT	SPOT	_ _ _ _	HYMN
e)	SEAL	<u>PEAR</u>	ROPE	PLOT	_ _ _ _	WAGS

SCORE   / 5

Phew, that was quite a lesson. Does your skull ache? Enjoy some rest and recreation
before going for **THE BIG ONE** … Test Paper 5.

Test Paper 5

▶ *Write the missing word of the second pair of words in the same way as the first pair has been made:*

1	slight	flight	sight	_____
2	crate	plate	crane	_____
3	quack	track	quick	_____
4	steep	feet	stoop	_____
5	bite	beat	white	_____

5 MARKS /5

▶ *Move one letter from the first word to the second word to give two new words:*

6	neat	toe	_____	_____
7	time	ice	_____	_____
8	king	litter	_____	_____
9	spite	car	_____	_____
10	guilt	cold	_____	_____

5 MARKS /5

▶ *Make a new word by adding a letter using the written clue:*

11	wan	_____	(need)
12	loud	_____	(water in the sky?)
13	read	_____	(a staple part of our diet)
14	pant	_____	(a green living thing)
15	tin	_____	(a pair)

5 MARKS /5

▶ *Unscramble these jumbled sentences:*

16 TIME IT IS FOR lunch yet? _____ lunch yet?

17 THE POSTMAN AT GROWLED THE DOG. _____

18 FLOWERS LOVES MOTHER My PINK best.

My _____ best.

19 MUSEUM THE CURATOR CHILDREN THE ASKED to behave.

_____ to behave.

20 Sir Lancelot THE TABLE WAS ROUND OF THE ONE OF KNIGHTS.

Sir Lancelot _____

5 MARKS /5

▶ *Work out these anagrams and write the correct word on the line:*

21 Mrs Jones went to the shops to buy milk, TREBUT and bread. _____

22 A CHANMECI mends car engines. _____

23 A DROLICOCE is a large reptile. _____

24 Water is a clear DQULII. _____

25 The roads will be icy as it is below ZERFEGIN. _____

26 Don't leave your LOWET on the floor! _____

27 The ship's sails billowed as it disappeared over the OZNOIRH. _____

28 An ambulance sped through the LAPOTISH gates. _____

29 My father has LEMRAMADA on his toast at breakfast. _____

30 A CTEBHRU sells meat. _____

10 MARKS   /10

▶ *Underline the most suitable word or number from each set of brackets so that the sentence or sum makes sense:*

31 (28 13 4) is greater than (8 4 12) x (8 6 10)

32 (7 5 3) x 5 (+ − x) 5 = (25 125 115)

33 Relying on its (cabbage, camera, camouflage), the (owl, elephant, fish) perched on a (berry, branch, burrow).

34 (Brushing, Combing, Teething) your (teeth, comb, hair) regularly will keep (it, them, that) white.

35 (15 33 19) (− x +) 18 = (2 23 15)

36 When Sally (climbed, fell, walked) down the stairs, (his, mine, her) mother came running from the (shops, race, kitchen).

37 It is (telling, clock, time) to (reach, go, fetch) to (bed, chair, curtain).

38 (Sixty, Sixteen, Six hundred) − (24 18 33) = (577 16 27)

39 Please (sit, eat, stand) up all (my, your, our) (cushions, vegetables, flowers), Sarah.

40 (26 47 36) divided by (4 6 9) = (3 6 12)

10 MARKS   /10

▶ *Write the same letter in the space so that it completes the first word and begins the second word:*

41 TRE__NDS

42 SPO__AME

43 MIL__IWI

44 SOA__REY

45 PIG__OUP

46 GOL__OOL

47 CLA__ULE

48 HAL__VER

49 SKE__OOD

50 GLA__ATE

10 MARKS   /10

▶ *Make a new word, taking away a letter and using the written clues:*

51 pride   _____   (sit astride a horse)

52 bright   _____   (correct)

53 tripe   _____   (stumble)

54 prince   _____   (cost)

55 staple   _____   (not fresh)

5 MARKS   /5

▶ *Put these words into alphabetical order:*

56 maid   laid   raid   said   paid

_____

57 sport   sponge   speck   spike   spade

_____

▶ *Put these items in size order, smallest first:*

58 newspaper   sweet wrapper   A4 paper   skyscraper

_____

59 hat box   horse box   matchbox   shoebox

_____

60 pebble   brick   sand grain   concrete block

_____

5 MARKS   /5

▶ *Make the missing word by following the same series of steps that created the underlined word:*

61	TIME	<u>MELT</u>	LOFT	PATH	_ _ _ _	ANON
62	TINY	<u>LENT</u>	ABLE	FEAR	_ _ _ _	PALE
63	RAGS	<u>GRIT</u>	ITEM	POOR	_ _ _ _	ENVY
64	SIFT	<u>FAST</u>	BALL	RIPE	_ _ _ _	HORN
65	BEEN	<u>LAMB</u>	CLAM	DRUM	_ _ _ _	PLEA
66	STUN	<u>NUTS</u>	CALM	BRAG	_ _ _ _	PILE
67	BALL	<u>LATE</u>	TAPE	WEFT	_ _ _ _	LOST
68	PALE	<u>LEAP</u>	TELL	PEST	_ _ _ _	FORT
69	TAME	<u>MINE</u>	NAIL	PINK	_ _ _ _	CHIN
70	MEAT	<u>EARL</u>	ROLE	STEP	_ _ _ _	NOTE

10 MARKS /10

▶ *Change one letter at a time to create a new word:*

71	SPOT	_ _ _ _	SLOW
72	CLAW	_ _ _ _	PLAN
73	FEEL	_ _ _ _	PEAL
74	FACE	_ _ _ _	LICE
75	NONE	_ _ _ _	CORE

5 MARKS /5

▶ *Find a letter that goes in front of all the given words to make new words:*

76	__runt	__rain	__eat
77	__age	__left	__art
78	__cross	__gain	__loud
79	__rain	__our	__ate
80	__rain	__round	__reed

5 MARKS /5

TOTAL = 80 MARKS   **Now turn to the answers on pages 87–88.**

▶ Relationships

Relationships between letters or numbers are really big in VR tests. 'What's a relationship?', you're probably wondering. Something like 'cornflakes is to box as milk is to ... bottle' – it's a kind of pattern you have to complete. These can take various forms.

LETTER PATTERNS ○ ○ ○

There are lots and lots of dull questions about relationships between letters – but they're easy to do once you know how.

6.1 | **Work out the relationship and fill in the gaps:**
A D is to E H as L O is to ___ .

• Megatip 981 is to have a copy of the alphabet in front of you. Usually the paper gives you one – if not, write one out very quickly <u>but take care you don't miss out any letters</u>.

• Once you've got your alphabet in front of you, map out the relationship on it like this, plotting each pair of letters:

A B C D E F G H I J K L M N O P Q R S T U V W X Y Z

• Quickly you can see there's a gap of two letters between each pair of letters, and that **EH** follows on directly from **AD**, so **LO** must be followed by **PS** – easy really. Now you can try – and we've thrown in a free alphabet for the price of the book ... a bargain really.

QUICK CHECK 1 ○–○–○

▷ *Work out the relationship and fill in the gaps:*

A B C D E F G H I J K L M N O P Q R S T U V W X Y Z

a)	L M	is to	N O	as	U V	is to	_____
b)	A C	is to	D F	as	I K	is to	_____
c)	G F	is to	E D	as	Z Y	is to	_____
d)	A D	is to	E H	as	I L	is to	_____
e)	K G	is to	F B	as	V R	is to	_____

SCORE ___ / 5

NUMBER PATTERNS ○ ○ ○

You get number patterns too – strange in a test of <u>verbal</u> reasoning, but there it is.

> **6.2**
>
> **Work out the relationship and fill in the gaps:**
>
> 1 2   is to   3 4   as   41 42   is to   _____

- It's the same basic method as with the letters – except that you can't write out all the numbers – it would take you ages …

- Look at the first two numbers: 1 2. On to the next two, 3 4. Easy – consecutive numbers. Move on: 41 42 – the missing ones are the next two numbers, so:

   Answer: 1 2   is to   3 4   as   41 42   is to   <u>43 44</u>

QUICK CHECK 2 ○○○

▶ *Work out the relationship and fill in the gaps:*

a)	7 8	is to	9 10	as	15 16	is to	_____
b)	15 17	is to	18 20	as	21 23	is to	_____
c)	90 80	is to	70 60	as	50 40	is to	_____
d)	26 29	is to	30 33	as	59 62	is to	_____
e)	35 32	is to	31 28	as	16 13	is to	_____

SCORE   / 5

PATTERNS USING LETTERS AND NUMBERS ○ ○ ○

Sometimes the examiners get a bit excited and ask you questions that involve both letters and numbers … The letters can be in capitals or lower case or both.

> **6.3**
>
> **Work out the relationship and fill in the gaps:**
>
> 14A   is to   21C   as   35E   is to   _____

- Work as before but you need to study the letters and numbers separately. (If the letter pattern looks really complicated, you may need an alphabet – here you don't.)

- A and C are two letters apart. So two letters on from E is G. 14 and 21 are seven apart. So you need to add seven to 35 as well. So:

   Answer: 14A   is to   21C   as   35E   is to   <u>42G</u>

QUICK CHECK 3

▶ *Work out the relationship and fill in the gaps:*

A B C D E F G H I J K L M N O P Q R S T U V W X Y Z

a) 6a   is to   11b   as   26f   is to   _____

b) n8o   is to   p9q   as   r10s   is to   _____

c) 99N   is to   88L   as   44D   is to   _____

d) 5h10   is to   15i20 as   25j30 is to   _____

e) zY3   is to   xW6   as   vU9   is to   _____

SCORE   / 5

WORD PATTERNS ○ ○ ○

Yes, we were bound to come back to words again in the end, so here goes ...

6.4   Wife is to husband as sister is to _____

You're looking for the connection so ... wife is the female part of a married couple, husband the male. The male version of a sister is a brother.

Sometimes, a choice is given like this:

6.4 Narrow is to _____ (wide, far, high) as high is to _____ (thin, low, near).

This is a bit trickier – you have to complete both relationships. Working from the left, check the two bits you do have: narrow and high – they have no relationship. You need to look for the relationship between narrow and the brackets first. So:

Answer: Narrow is to <u>wide</u> as high is to <u>low</u>.

Although this example is about opposites, <u>the relationship may be about similars</u>, as here:

6.4 Thin is to _____ (fat, slender, tall) as short is to _____ (thin, small, large).

You start by checking thin is to ... fat. This looks OK – they're opposites. But short is to ...there's no tall here – so the relationship can't be about opposites. Look again and you see it must be about similars:

Answer: Thin is to <u>slender</u> as short is to <u>small</u>.

QUICK CHECK 4

a) Dog is to kennel as horse is to _____.

b) (Eye, Boot, Blood) _____ is to human as (sap, petal, leaf) _____ is to plant.

c) Cushion is to chair as pillow is to _____.

d) Bird is to _____ (fly, wing, feathers) as fish is to _____ (shark, gills, swim).

e) Knife is to _____ (sharp, blade, cut) as fork is to _____ (blunt, spoon, prongs).

SCORE / 5

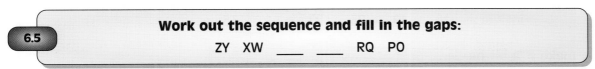

Quick check 4 answers: a) stable; b) Blood sap; c) bed; d) fly swim; e) blade prongs

SEQUENCES OF LETTERS

Sometimes you get sequences of letters like this:

6.5 **Work out the sequence and fill in the gaps:**
EF ___ MN QR UV ___

A sequence is a pattern that repeats itself or follows in a chain. You need the use the old alphabet again – if it isn't given, write it out. (We're generous souls – so here it is.) Map out what's given on the alphabet.

A B C D E F G H I J K L M N O P Q R S T U V W X Y Z

EF are consecutive letters, so the pattern appears to be going forwards. Because the second pairing is missing, go to the third and fourth. MN, consecutive letters again, and QR. Count how many letters are missing between MN and QR. Answer: two. Look between QR and UV – two also. Add two onto UV and the next pairing will be YZ. Go back to the first gap. EF add two and the missing pair is IJ.

Answer: EF <u>IJ</u> MN QR UV <u>YZ</u>

Here's another to look at:

6.5 **Work out the sequence and fill in the gaps:**
ZY XW ___ ___ RQ PO

Map it on the alphabet and you'll see that the letters are going <u>backwards</u>. Follow along from Z, working to the left, as it is going backwards in pairs. The next one after XW is UT then SR. So:

ZY XW <u>VU</u> <u>TS</u> RQ PO

Just so you're bored rigid with these, here's one more:

LESSON 6

6.5 AZ CX EV ___ ___ KP

It's easier than it looks. The letters are taken from both ends of the alphabet at the same time. **AZ** are the ends. Then there's a jump missing out **B** and **Y**. Check it all against the alphabet and you'll get:

AZ   CX   EV   <u>GT</u>   <u>IR</u>   KP

QUICK CHECK 5

a) BC	EF	HI	___	NO	___
b) Zy	Xw	Vu	___	___	Po
c) VU	___	___	ML	JI	GF
d) ___	EV	FU	GT	HS	___
e) ___	___	JM	NQ	RU	VY

SCORE   / 5

Quick check 5 answers: a) KL QR (simple forwards, missing one out between each pairing);
b) Ts Rq (simple backwards. Watch out for capitals and lower case);
c) SR Po (simple backwards, missing one out between each pairing);
d) DW IR (working inwards from both ends of alphabet); e) BE FI (forwards, missing two out in the pair)

SEQUENCES OF NUMBERS

You get the same thing with numbers – once examiners get a dull idea they don't like to let go of it, so here goes …

6.6 Work out the sequence and fill in the gaps:
15   19   23   ___   31   ___

Work from the left … where have you heard that before? Start by looking at the gap between the numbers – then it's easy:

15   19   23   ___   31   ___

It looks like a pattern of adding four. Check by adding four to **23**, which is **27**. Then add four more … **31** is right – so complete the pattern.

Answer: 15   19   23   <u>27</u>   31   <u>35</u>

Let's make it a bit harder.

6.6   2   4   8   ___   ___   64

Try mapping the pattern:

2   4   8   ___   ___   64

58

The differences are 2, 4 ... the next number could be 6 (going up by two each time) ... or it could be 8 (doubling). Try each answer and see which gets you to 64. The answer is:

2   4   8   <u>16</u>   <u>32</u>   64

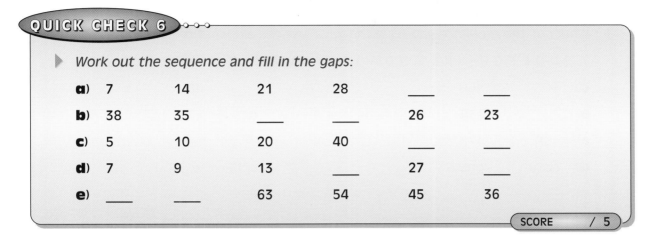

QUICK CHECK 6

▶ *Work out the sequence and fill in the gaps:*

a)	7	14	21	28	___	___
b)	38	35	___	___	26	23
c)	5	10	20	40	___	___
d)	7	9	13	___	27	___
e)	___	___	63	54	45	36

SCORE   / 5

SEQUENCES OF LETTERS AND NUMBERS

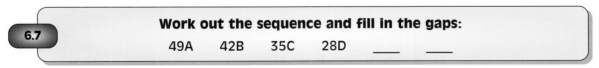

Finally you get round to sequences that combine both letters and numbers.

6.7   **Work out the sequence and fill in the gaps:**

49A   42B   35C   28D   ___   ___

The trick is: <u>you have to deal with the letters and numbers separately</u>. Numbers first – what's the pattern?

49   42   35   28

Easy – going down in sevens. What about the letters?

A   B   C   D   E

Easy, going up one letter at a time, so:

49A   42B   35C   28D   <u>21E</u>   <u>14F</u>

Just to make sure you've got this here's a really tough one.

6.7   **Work out the sequence and fill in the gaps:**

a17Z   b18Y   c20X   d23W   ___   ___

Start from the left. There're three things here – lower case letters (a, b, c), numbers (17, 18, 20), upper case letters (Z, Y, X). Do each one separately:

Lower case letters: a b c d ... next two? Peasy ... e f

Numbers: 17 18 20 23 ... pattern? Increasing by one each time, so: 27, 32

Upper case letters: Z Y X W ... going back one each time. Next two ...V U

Put it all together and you get:

a17Z   b18Y   c20X   d23W   e27V   f32U

QUICK CHECK 7

▶ Work out the sequence and fill in the gaps. Use the alphabet to help you.

A B C D E F G H I J K L M N O P Q R S T U V W X Y Z

a)	8G	16H	___	32J	___	48L
b)	___	e34	___	c28	b25	a22
c)	15F	17H	19J	21L	___	___
d)	cd59	gh54	___	___	st39	wx34
e)	___	___	C16X	D12W	E8V	F4U

SCORE   / 5

(upside-down) **Quick check 7 answers:** a) 24I 40K (numbers upwards in 8's, letters in order); b) f37 d31 (numbers downwards in 3's, letters backwards in order); c) 23N 25P (numbers upwards in 2's, letters forwards in 2's); d) kl49 op44 (numbers downwards in 5's, letters omitting two between pairs); e) A24Z B20Y (letters in order, numbers downwards in 4's, letters backwards in order)

And now of course it's test paper time again!

Test Paper 6

minutes

▶ Work out the relationship and fill in the gaps:

1 13 14   is to   15 16   as   24 25   is to _____
2 39 44   is to   45 50   as   55 60   is to _____
3 010   is to   020   as   030   is to _____
4 24 26   is to   27 29   as   53 55   is to _____
5 47 41   is to   40 34   as   33 27   is to _____

5 MARKS   /5

▶ Work out the relationship and fill in the gaps:

6 14c   is to   21d   as   28e   is to _____
7 m6n   is to   o5p   as   q4r   is to _____
8 24x   is to   22w   as   14s   is to _____
9 4V8   is to   12U16   as   20T24   is to _____
10 Z48Y   is to   X40W   as   V32U   is to _____

5 MARKS   /5

▶ *Find one letter that will complete and start each set of words:*

11	THI __ AIL	SPI__OTE
12	FIN __ EAL	SPE__ EER
13	CLI __ URE	CLA__ INT
14	FLA __ INY	SUI__ RIM
15	PLA __OLK	PON__ARN
16	TRI __ILK	PRA__ICE
17	GRU __ULK	BUL__ARK
18	PAT __UGE	BUS__AZE
19	TAN __ING	BAC__NOT
20	HEE __EFT	KIL__OVE

10 MARKS   /10

▶ *Change one letter at a time to create a new word:*

21	HUNK	_ _ _ _	MONK
22	DAME	_ _ _ _	HAZE
23	BLOW	_ _ _ _	CROW
24	LEFT	_ _ _ _	BENT
25	HOOP	_ _ _ _	ROOF

5 MARKS   /5

▶ *Work out the relationship and fill in the gaps:*

26	E F	is to	G H	as	N O	is to	_____
27	R T	is to	U W	as	H J	is to	_____
28	N M	is to	L K	as	X W	is to	_____
29	C G	is to	H L	as	M Q	is to	_____
30	Z W	is to	V S	as	R O	is to	_____

5 MARKS   /5

▶ *Work out the relationship and fill in the gaps:*

31 Sock is to foot as glove is to _____.

32 Beetle is to six legs as cow is to _____ legs.

33 Finger is to toe as hand is to _____.

34 Aunt is to niece as uncle is to _____.

35 Beetroot is to red as sprouts are to _____.

36 Loud is to quiet as wet is to _____.

37 Evening is to _____ (twilight, sunset, home) as morning is to

_____ (sunrise, breakfast, toothpaste).

TURN OVER ▶

38 Studs are to _____ (football boots, horses, earrings) as spikes are to _____ (hedgehogs, golf shoes, iron railings).

39 _____ (Crow, Raven, Rook) is to chess as _____ (diamonds, emeralds, rubies) are to cards.

40 Flour is to _____ (baker, bread, vase) as sand is to _____ (seaside, cement, castle).

⎯⎯⎯⎯⎯⎯⎯⎯⎯⎯⎯⎯⎯ 10 MARKS /10

▶ *Make a new word by taking away a letter using the written clue:*

41 SPEND (dispatch) _____

42 CEASE (container) _____

43 SCONE (a 3D shape) _____

44 MEANT (flesh) _____

45 THICKET (piece of paper or card) _____

⎯⎯⎯⎯⎯⎯⎯⎯⎯⎯⎯⎯⎯ 5 MARKS /5

▶ *Underline the word that cannot be made from the long word:*

46 PRICELESS creep slice crisp crease

47 BEAUTIFUL flute about leaf fable

48 CREATURE crust tear cure rear

49 CALCULATE lace crate tall teal

50 PRINCESS crisp rinse spine cease

⎯⎯⎯⎯⎯⎯⎯⎯⎯⎯⎯⎯⎯ 5 MARKS /5

▶ *Write the missing word of the second pair of words in the same way as the first pair of words has been made:*

51 fill will fell _____

52 spate spook hate _____

53 cloudy cloudier shady _____

54 fate mate fatter _____

55 sheep sheet cheap _____

⎯⎯⎯⎯⎯⎯⎯⎯⎯⎯⎯⎯⎯ 5 MARKS /5

▶ *Underline the two words that are made from the same letters:*

56 table stable bleat sleet blast

57 pearl pillar petal pleat plait

58 stool ghost tools toast tooth

59 those shoot sheet shoal these

60   parted   pasted   passed   depart   spared

▶ *Work out the sequence and fill in the gaps:*

A B C D E F G H I J K L M N O P Q R S T U V W X Y Z

61 BD	FH	____	NP	RT	____
62 ____	____	TS	QP	NM	KJ
63 Ac	Ce	Eg	____	Ik	____
64 AD	EH	____	MP	____	UX
65 AZ	BY	CX	____	____	FU

5 MARKS   /5

▶ *Work out the sequence and fill in the gaps:*

A B C D E F G H I J K L M N O P Q R S T U V W X Y Z

66 ____	12Y	14X	16W	18V	____
67 B35	D32	____	____	J23	L20
68 31a	35c	____	____	47i	51k
69 ab10	____	ij14	mn16	____	uv20
70 ____	____	c8X	d6W	e4V	f2U

5 MARKS   /5

▶ *Find a letter that goes in front of all the given words to make new words:*

71	__peak	__quid	__teak
72	__rail	__rapped	__weak
73	__are	__rave	__east
74	__host	__rate	__litter
75	__ash	__rayon	__rack

5 MARKS   /5

▶ *Work out the sequence and fill in the gaps:*

76 5	10	15	____	25	____
77 39	35	____	27	____	19
78 3	6	12	____	48	____
79 34	24	16	10	____	____
80 ____	____	24	18	12	6

5 MARKS   /5

63

TOTAL = 80 MARKS   **Now turn to the answers on pages 88–90.**

LESSON 7 • Substitution

▶ Substitution

What's substitution? Something that happens in footie matches, I hear you say. Well yes ... it's also a VR trick – and much more exciting. Usually you have to swap letters for numbers, or the other way round, to get the answer. Accept no substitute ...

Substitution questions are very straightforward if you follow the rules. Here letters are given numerical values.

7.1
If a = 5 e = 3 r = 2 s = 1 t = 4 what are the totals of these words?

| rat | ___ | rest | ___ | tea | ___ |

| set | ___ | star | ___ |

In a test, rather than rely on mental arithmetic, write the values down. It is always safer. Look at the first word rat. r = 2, a = 5, t = 4. Add them together: 11. Repeat for rest. r = 2, e = 3, s = 1, t = 4. Altogether? Answer is 10. Repeat for the others – no problem.

| rat | 11 | rest | 10 | tea | 12 |
| set | 8 | star | 12 | | |

A variation on the same theme is ...

7.1
If a = 3 b = 6 c = 2 d = 10 e = 5 work out these sums. Write your answer as a letter.

$$a + c = \underline{\quad} \qquad b \div a = \underline{\quad}$$
$$d - e = \underline{\quad} \qquad ce = \underline{\quad}$$

Take the first sum, a + c. a = 3, c = 2. 3 + 2 = 5. The answer must be written as a letter. e = 5, so e is the answer. Then they're easy. <u>Don't forget to turn your answer back into a letter at the end.</u>

b ÷ a is 6 ÷ 3 = 2 **Answer:** c. d – e is 10 – 5 = 5 **Answer:** e.
ce is 2 x 5 = 10 **Answer:** d.

QUICK CHECK 1

▶ If a = 5 e = 4 s = 3 y = 2 t = 1 what are the totals of these words?

a) yes ___

b) sat ___

c) sea ___

d) eat ___

e) easy ___

> If a = 2 b = 4 c = 12 d = 6 e = 3 *work out these sums. Write your answer as a letter.*

f) d – b = _____

g) b + d + a = _____

h) c – d = _____

i) c divided by e = _____

j) ad = _____

SCORE   / 10

▶ Codes

CODES IN NUMBERS ○ ○ ○

7.2

If the code for BREAKS is 743512 work out these codes/words:

521 _____   4513 _____

BAR _____   AREA _____

Work from left to right and take it slowly, one letter at a time. If the paper does not set the words and numbers out under each other, do so yourself, like this:

B R E A K S
7 4 3 5 1 2

This makes it easier to match them accurately. Write down the answer as you go along. So:

5 = A 2 = S 1 = K. Put them together – ASK. Do the same for 4513.
B = 7 A = 5 R = 4. Put them together – 754. Do the same for AREA.

521   ASK   4513   RAKE
BAR   754   AREA   5435

Here's another version of number codes. In the example below, you have been given the answers. You just have to work out which goes where.

7.2

The codes for these words have been mixed up.
Write the correct code under each word.

BEND	BOOK	NODE	KNOB
2118	8312	2634	3146

BEND	BOOK	NODE	KNOB
_ _ _ _	_ _ _ _	_ _ _ _	_ _ _ _

Now work out the code for: BOND

_ _ _ _

• This is trickier and needs careful study. Read the words carefully. <u>The key is to look for words which have the same letter in the same position.</u> So, two words begin with B. Look at the codes to find two that begin with the same number. Two begin with 2. Just check that the other two words don't begin with another letter the same. No? Write these letters in the right place on the answer line under the B's.

• Now look again. Two words have O in the second position. Find two numbers the same in the second position ... 1. Also B<u>OO</u>K has double O, so that must have 11 in the middle. That means 2118 must be BOOK, and 8 must be K. You've now got enough clues to finish off the set:

BEND	BOOK	NODE	KNOB
2634	2118	3146	8312

• BOND can be worked out letter by letter using the ones you know. So:

BOND
2134

CODES IN LETTERS ₀ ₀ ₀

• You also get letter codes – where one letter stands for another one as in all the best spy films. These are a bit more confusing but they're not much harder if you're careful.

7.2   **The code for COLDER is PZRNXF.   What is FZRX?** _____

Treat this type of question in exactly the same way as the numbers. Write one under the other for starters.

COLDER
PZRNXF

So with FZRX, F = R Z = O R = L X = E. Put them together: ROLE.

Sometimes the examiners try to make things really hard.

7.2   **The code for COOL is DPPM.   What is the code for WARM?** _____

• You quickly realise that COOL and WARM have no shared letters ... help! The first reaction is to think 'how on earth do I do this?' – and panic ... but don't. Instead coolly write one word under the other.

COOL
DPPM

• There is a pattern in the code you can reuse. Look carefully. C = D, O = P, L = M. Spotted it? Yes, the letters in the code are one after the actual letters. If it looks complicated map it on an alphabet:

A B C D E F G H I J K L M N O P Q R S T U V W X Y Z

So in WARM, W becomes X, A becomes B and so on:

Answer: The code for WARM is XBSN.

CODES IN SYMBOLS ○ ○ ○

This is just another feeble attempt by examiners to fool you. Chuckle to yourself then treat them just like number codes.

7.2

The code for BLAST is * % £ $!

Decipher this word: $ % £ * _____

• You may want to write it as before, but be careful because symbols can be a little harder to write:

B L A S T
* % £ $!

• Find the first sign in the new symbol code: $ ... you'll quickly see it's **S**. Then do the rest. So:

$ % £ * is SLAB

Now here's a chance for you to practise all your code skills ... good luck, secret agent!

QUICK CHECK 2 ○ ○ ○

▶ *If the code for TEAMS is 71263 work out these codes/words:*

a) 312   _____

b) TAME   _____

▶ *The codes for these words have been mixed up. Write the correct code under each word.*

c) DEAR   READ   RAID   What is RIDE ?
6432   2546   6542

_____   _____   _____   _____

▶ *The code for DREAM is XCWLZ. Work out these words:*

d) CLZ   _____

e) ZLXW   _____

▶ *The code for SPOON is RONNM. What is:*

f) FORK   _____

g) CUP   _____

▶ *The code for FEARS is < £ * & > Decipher the following words:*

h) < * &   _____

i) > £ *   _____

j) > * < £   _____

SCORE   / 10

7 ▶ Logic

Logic's about thinking straight ... which is what all VR's about really. In logic questions you have to answer questions using the information you have been given. <u>These questions can be time consuming. In a test situation, beware of spending lots of time on these unless there are lots of marks too!</u>

They come in various forms. Here are some examples:

> **7.3**
>
> Mrs Smith has 4 children.
> Sara is 2 years younger than Jade.
> Peter, the oldest, is 10 and 3 years older than Jade.
> The baby, Jack, cries a lot.
> **How old is Sara?**

The key here is to read carefully – and to quickly ignore useless information. It's irrelevant how much the baby cries – so just ignore its wails! Concentrate on what you do know. Write it down in the margin. The most important fact is the actual age of any child. Peter is 10. If he is 3 years older than Jade, she must be 7. Sara is 2 years younger than Jade, so:

Answer: Sara is 5

It's an easy question but needs quite a lot of working out for just one mark. If you were in a test and running short of time, this would be the one to miss out unless you could see the answer very quickly. Here's another ...

> **7.3**
>
> FISH LIVE IN WATER   WATER IS A LIQUID.
> **Underline the statement which is true.**
> Fish are liquid.
> All liquids are water.
> Fish live in a liquid.

You need to deduce what makes sense, given the information that you have. The fact that water is a liquid does not make fish one also. Fish are solid! The second statement is also rubbish. There are other liquids besides water. The third is the answer. Fish live in water, which is a liquid, so fish live in a liquid.

And just to make sure you've seen all the logic you'll ever want ...

> **7.3**
>
> A cat has six kittens.
> Half the litter have green eyes, the others have yellow.   Two are ginger toms.
> All three females have yellow eyes, one is tabby.
> Two kittens are black and white.   One is tortoiseshell with yellow eyes.
>
> **1** What sex is the tortoiseshell kitten? _____
> **2** What colour eyes do have the ginger kittens have? _____
> **3** Write the sex and correct eye colour for each of the black-and-white kittens.
>
> _____   _____

It is unusual to find so many questions on a logic question.
Work through carefully and you should gain easy marks.
1 As the tortoiseshell has yellow eyes it must be female
(line 4).
2 The gingers are boys and have green eyes (line 2).
3 Two gingers = male; one tabby and one tortoiseshell = female.
Therefore: one black-and-white male with green eyes, the other
female with yellow eyes.

QUICK CHECK 3

a) David, Max, Tom and Chris sat an exam, which had a pass mark of 50%.
Max passed the exam, and Tom scored 66%.
Underline the statement which must be true.
David and Chris failed the exam.
Max got the highest percentage.
Tom passed the exam.
Tom scored more than David.

b) Sally runs a riding school.
3 of the 10 ponies, Daisy, Dandy and Don, are very old and need hay,
carrots and a bucket of food.
Snowy, Guzzle, Jim and Poppy just have hay.
Bess is allergic to hay. She has lots of carrots and a bucket of food instead.
Magpie has hay and carrots.
Bob is thin. He doesn't like carrots but he has everything else.
How many ponies have a bucket of food?

c) Ardlour, Bertham, Conley and Deeson are seaside resorts.
Ardlour, Deeson and Bertham have ice cream stalls.
Conley, Deeson and Ardlour have lifeguards.
Deeson, Bertham and Conley have restaurants.
All the resorts sell postcards, except Bertham, which has a very small beach.
1 Which resort has all the amenities? _____
2 Which resort has a lifeguard but not an ice cream stall? _____
3 Which resort sells postcards but does not have a restaurant? _____

SCORE _____ / 5

OK, you've now covered everything – here's your chance to practise it all. Actually
here're two chances ... Test Papers 7 and 8 provide two final goes at a complete range
of VR skills. Make sure you've had a good break before trying one of these papers.
And when you've done both you could go to the full realistic 11+ practice experience
with one of the books of practice papers featured on the back cover.

▶ If f = 1 g = 2 h = 3 i = 4 j = 6 work out these sums. Write your answer as a letter.

    1 j − i = ____

    2 g + h + f = ____

    3 i − h = ____

    4 gh = ____

    5 j divided by h = ____

5 MARKS   /5

▶ Make the missing word by following the same series of steps that created the underlined word:

6	TYPE	<u>COPY</u>	COIL	VETO	_ _ _ _	RASP
7	BEST	<u>BARS</u>	PART	FATE	_ _ _ _	BELL
8	QUIT	<u>TRIP</u>	PRAY	OXEN	_ _ _ _	DEAD
9	BATH	<u>HARE</u>	RENT	WART	_ _ _ _	KEPT
10	CUTE	<u>CART</u>	TARN	VAIN	_ _ _ _	EASY

5 MARKS   /5

▶ If r = 6 s = 3 t = 2 o = 1 e = 5 what are the totals of these words?

    11 roe   ____

    12 sort   ____

    13 toes   ____

    14 sore   ____

    15 toss   ____

5 MARKS   /5

▶ Make a new word by adding a letter, using the written clue:

    16 rush   _____ (broom)

    17 tick   _____ (not thin)

    18 sauce _____ (goes under a cup)

    19 thin   _____ (to ponder)

    20 spot   _____ (games)

5 MARKS   /5

Make a new word by taking away a letter, using the written clue:

21 blush _____ (abundant)

22 twitter _____ (giggle)

23 grasp _____ (pant)

24 wriggle _____ (a line with curves)

25 gnash _____ (cut)

5 MARKS /5

Work out the relationship and fill in the gaps:

26 25 22 is to 21 18 as 13 10 is to _____

27 30 40 is to 50 60 as 70 80 is to _____

28 61 59 is to 57 55 as 53 51 is to _____

29 33 44 is to 55 66 as 11 22 is to _____

30 7 77 is to 6 66 as 5 55 is to _____

5 MARKS /5

Move one letter from the first word to the second word to give two new words:

31 HOOT SON _____ _____

32 PLAY WAY _____ _____

33 TRIM WIN _____ _____

34 SPLIT WAR _____ _____

35 CHIRP BOOM _____ _____

5 MARKS /5

Work out the relationship and fill in the gaps:

36 Cub is to wolf as gosling is to _____.

37 Legs are to walking as lungs are to _____.

38 Piano is to keys as guitar is to _____.

39 Laugh is to _____ (grimace, chuckle, glare) as scowl is to _____ (guffaw, chortle, glare).

40 Eggs are to _____ (meringues, hens, sausages) as cocoa is to _____ (coconuts, chocolate, butter).

5 MARKS /5

TURN OVER ▶

▶ If the code for SPENT is 61432 work out these codes/words:

41 TEN   _____

42 1426   _____

▶ The codes for these words have been mixed up. Write the correct code under each word:

43 CORN   **44** RACE   **45** ACRE   **46** What is NEAR?
      6431   4235   3641

      _____   _____   _____   _____

▶ The code for SCHOOL is UEJQQN. What are these codes/words?

47 BOOK   _____

48 RGP   _____

▶ The code for CRATE is @ ~ # * ^ . Decipher the following words:

49 @ # ~ ^   _____

50 * ~ # @ ^   _____

10 MARKS   /10

▶ Work out the relationship and fill in the gaps:

A B C D E F G H I J K L M N O P Q R S T U V W X Y Z

51 4Z   is to   8Y   as   12X   is to   _____

52 e6f   is to   g8h   as   i10j   is to   _____

53 50n   is to   40p   as   30r   is to   _____

54 ZA30   is to   YB25   as   XC20   is to   _____

55 3W6   is to   9U12   as   15S18   is to   _____

5 MARKS   /5

▶ Change one letter at a time to create a new word:

56 SORT   _ _ _ _   _ _ _ _   BARE

57 FOOT   _ _ _ _   _ _ _ _   SLOW

58 MORE   _ _ _ _   _ _ _ _   MINT

59 POND   _ _ _ _   _ _ _ _   FORK

60 WILL   _ _ _ _   _ _ _ _   SALT

5 MARKS   /5

▶ *Work out the sequence and fill in the gaps:*

61	3	6	___	12	___	18
62	25	___	21	19	17	___
63	___	___	30	40	50	60
64	8	12	___	___	24	28
65	___	49	42	35	___	21

5 MARKS /5

66–67 The gorillas at Natchett Zoo are fussy eaters.
Fruli will only eat leaves and oranges.
Zulu likes leaves, bananas, dates and apples.
Kong only likes bananas and oranges.
Tubby lives up to his name and eats everything that the others eat
except oranges which he throws at the keeper.

Which gorilla eats bananas but not dates? _____

2 MARKS /2

68–69 On a new estate, 64 of the 100 houses have been sold. All the 3-bedroom
houses have been sold and some of the 4-bedroom houses.

Underline the statement that must be true.

All the 2-bedroom houses have been sold.
None of the 3-bedroom houses are for sale.
All the houses are made of brick.
There are 36 4-bedroom houses still for sale.

2 MARKS /2

Tom, Dick, Harry, Fred, Sally and Donna all play musical instruments.
Tom, Donna and Fred play the violin.
Sally, Harry and Tom play the clarinet.
Dick, Fred and Sally play the trumpet.
All the children play in the orchestra except one who plays only one
instrument.
Sally and Tom also play this instrument.

70–71 Who plays all the instruments except the trumpet? _____

72–73 Fred would like to play another instrument. He is thinking of taking up
the one which Sally plays as one of her instruments.
Which instrument would he like to take up? _____

74–75 Who is not in the orchestra? _____

6 MARKS /6

7

Natasha, Boris, Olga, Ivan, Tanya and Misha are students at a languages institute in Moscow.

Natasha speaks French, German, English and Russian.
Boris speaks Arabic, French and Russian.
Olga speaks Russian, English and French.
Ivan speaks Polish, German and Russian.
Tanya speaks Russian, Chinese and English.
Misha speaks Russian, Spanish, French and English.

76–77 *Underline the statements which are true.*

They all learned to speak foreign languages by listening to foreign radio stations.
They all speak English.
They all speak at least two languages.
They all want to be cosmonauts.
None of them speaks Spanish.
They all speak Russian.

78 Who speaks German but not Polish? _____

79 Who speaks French and other languages but not English? _____

80 Who speaks English but not French? _____

5 MARKS   /5

TOTAL = 80 MARKS   **Now turn to the answers on pages 90–92.**

- -

Test Paper 8 .... minutes

▶ *If a = 5 b = 6 c = 2 d = 10 e = 4 work out these sums. Write your answer as a letter.*

1 d – b =   ____

2 d divided by c = ____

3 ac = ____

4 b + e = ____

5 ae divided by d = ____

5 MARKS   /5

▶ *Change one letter at a time to create a new word:*

6 SLIP   _ _ _ _   _ _ _ _   STAB

7 CAVE   _ _ _ _   _ _ _ _   LINE

8 RATS   _ _ _ _   _ _ _ _   PITY

9 DIVE   _ _ _ _   _ _ _ _   LIFT

10 CLAY   _ _ _ _   _ _ _ _   SPAT

5 MARKS   /5

▶ *Unscramble these jumbled sentences:*

11 YOU ARE FEELING HOW today?

_____today?

12 MR BROWN down ROAD walked THE HANDS HOLDING AND MRS.

_____ walked down_____

13 SIZE TWICE MY GOLDFISH YOURS IS THE OF.

_____

14 PURPLE Red and BLUE MAKE TOGETHER MIXED.

Red and _____

15 my MOUSE FROZEN THE COMPUTER on HAS.

_____ on my _____

| 5 MARKS | /5 |

▶ *If a = 2 e = 3 l = 4 p = 5 t = 6 what are the totals of these words?*

16 pat   _____

17 tale   _____

18 lap   _____

19 teal   _____

20 plate   _____

| 5 MARKS | /5 |

▶ *Underline the word that can be made from the long word:*

21 SLIMMING   swim   mini   lime   slug

22 SAUCEPAN   scene   pant   race   pace

23 PRINCESS   sense   since   pinch   score

▶ *Underline the word that cannot be made from the long word:*

24 PATIENCE   nice   tape   nets   cane

25 TRAILER   real   liar   earl   train

26 ADVANCE   dance   cane   acre   nave

| 6 MARKS | /6 |

▶ *Work out the relationship and fill in the gaps.*

A B C D E F G H I J K L M N O P Q R S T U V W X Y Z

27	3a	is to	4b	as	5c	is to	_____
28	10Z	is to	12Y	as	16W	is to	_____
29	15q	is to	20s	as	45x	is to	_____
30	aB8	is to	cD11	as	iJ15	is to	_____
31	99h6	is to	88i5	as	55m8	is to	_____
32	az16	is to	by20	as	cx24	is to	_____
33	W81p	is to	V72q	as	U63r	is to	_____

7 MARKS   /7

▶ *If the code for SWEAT is 37204 work out these codes/words:*

34 420   _____

35 WEST   _____

36 70342   _____

▶ *The codes for these words have been mixed up. Write the correct code under each word.*

37 SOCK	**38** KIOSK	**39** COST
50235	6234	3265
_____	_____	_____

40 What is the code for TICK? _____

▶ *If the code for FIERCE is & * % $ @ % then what are these words when deciphered?*

41 $ * @ %   _____

42 & * $ %   _____

43 $ % % &   _____

10 MARKS   /10

▶ *Find a four-letter word that can be added to the letters in capitals to make a larger word:*

44 The trickster SLED him out of his money. _____

45 A sore throat makes it difficult to SOW. _____

46 He WA his own clothes. _____

47 The soldier was awarded a medal for his BRY. _____

48 PL close the door behind you. _____

5 MARKS   /5

▶ *Work out the relationship and fill in the gaps:*

49 Niece is to nephew as sister is to _____.

50 Elbow is to arm as knee is to _____.

51 Drake is to duck as gander is to _____.

52 Boat is to boathouse as car is to _____.

53 Madrid is to Spain as Paris is to _____.

54 Daytime is to _____ (light, sunshine, flowers) as night time is to _____ (wind, stars, dark).

55 Yellow and blue are to _____ (lilac, green, purple) as yellow and red are to _____ (pink, lemon, orange).

56 Arrow is to _____ (quiver, bow, wound) as sword is to _____ (armour, scabbard, fight).

57 Street is to _____ (road, lamp, road signs) as stream is to _____ (bridge, boulder, brook).

58 Button is to _____ (chocolate, buttonhole, coat) as zip is to _____ (trousers, cotton, button).

────────────────────────────────── 10 MARKS /10

Dangle, the seven-spot ladybird, and his wife, Mangle, had thirteen children who were known by their numbers. Numbers 1 to 7 were males and 8 to 13 were females.
Only one of the babies grew to adulthood.
1, 3, 7 and 9 were eaten by birds.
11 and 13 drowned in a puddle.
One ladybird baby got stuck in a spider's web.
Three females were trodden on by a cow.
Number 2 was very greedy and died from eating too many greenfly.
Number 5 was caught by a small boy and was kept in a jam jar but, unfortunately, he forgot to feed him.

59 How many of the children were female? _____

60 How many were eaten by birds? _____

61 What sex was the ladybird who died in the spider's web? _____

62 What sex was the survivor? _____

63 What happened to Number 8? _____

64 If Number 4 got stuck in the spider's web, what number was the survivor?

_____

────────────────────────────────── 6 MARKS /6

Underline the pair of words most similar in meaning:

65	cup/mug	tea bag/teapot	jug/saucer
66	rubber/ruler	pencil/pen	sharpener/felt pen
67	brick/cement	stone/rock	paint/brush
68	right/left	lost/hidden	correct/right
69	pale/bright	sunny/cloudy	pail/bucket
70	hot/cold	tepid/warm	warm/cool

6 MARKS   /6

Work out the sequence and fill in the gaps:

A B C D E F G H I J K L M N O P Q R S T U V W X Y Z

71	FG	IJ	LM	____	RS	____
72	Wv	Ut	____	Qp	____	MI
73	____	____	mn	qr	uv	yz
74	ZA	____	XC	____	VE	UF
75	abc	bcd	cde	def	____	____
76	12A	15D	____	21J	24M	____
77	____	by14	____	dw28	ev35	fu42
78	96	48	24	____	____	3
79	65	____	57	____	49	45
80	____	4Jj	8Kk	16Ll	32Mm	____

10 MARKS   /10

TOTAL = 80 MARKS   Now turn to the answers on pages 92–93.

Answers

MARKING YOUR WORK ∘ ∘ ∘

Now you need to mark your work. You'll find that next to each answer or group of answers there's a tutorial giving you tips on the answer. We've also referred you back to the test type if you want to check up how it's done.

▶ **1.2** p.9

> **1** open closed
> Read the question! Make sure you do opposites.

HOW DID YOU DO? ∘ ∘ ∘

When you've marked your work do the following:

* record your score if you want on the record sheet on pages 94–95.
* follow the ideas below on improving your performance. Use the flow chart to help you.

Was your score as you expected? Did you have time to finish? Were there certain question types you did badly? Now is the time to learn from your mistakes.

If you finished:

* think how you could improve your score. Did you rush certain areas? If so, slow down a bit next time, read the question carefully at least twice and think more carefully. Do not guess wildly.

* Did your checking pay off? It may be hard to see where you've gone wrong. Take it calmly. If you didn't rush madly the chances are you were right first time round. Look instead for questions that you were less confident about. Just have a sensible guess rather than leave a blank space.

If you didn't finish:

* Firstly – don't worry. This is very common when you start to do timed tests.
* If you got right nearly all you did do that's great. Now you need to try to speed up a bit. 40 out of 50 is a high percentage score – but remember that the paper is marked out of 80. You must tackle more questions to get a good score. Complete the rest of the paper now and mark it. Here are some ideas for speeding up.
  – Pick the questions you know you can complete relatively easily.
  – You do not have to do the questions in order.
  – Come back to the ones you find more time consuming at the end.
  – Be strict over the amount of time you spend on each group of questions. To help you to gauge this, look and see how many marks are allocated.
  – Always try to put an answer in, and make a sensible guess if necessary.

Improving your score:
Use the flow chart on the next page to help you.

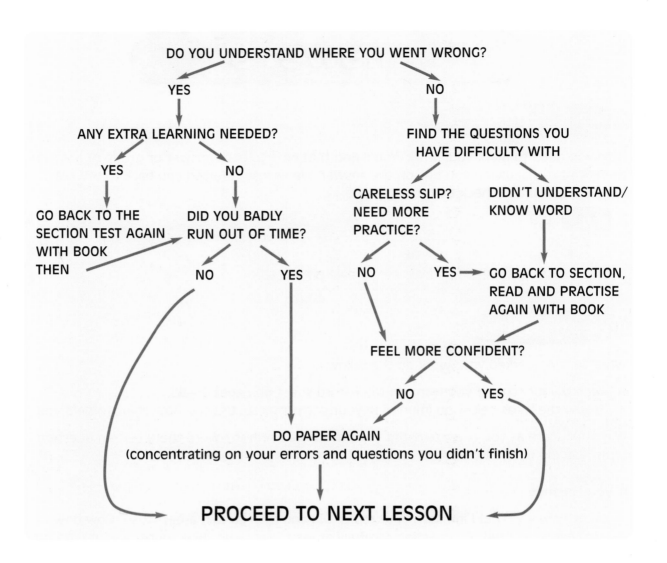

DO YOU UNDERSTAND WHERE YOU WENT WRONG?

YES → ANY EXTRA LEARNING NEEDED?

YES → GO BACK TO THE SECTION TEST AGAIN WITH BOOK THEN

NO → DID YOU BADLY RUN OUT OF TIME?

NO / YES

NO → FIND THE QUESTIONS YOU HAVE DIFFICULTY WITH

CARELESS SLIP? NEED MORE PRACTICE?

DIDN'T UNDERSTAND/ KNOW WORD

NO / YES → GO BACK TO SECTION, READ AND PRACTISE AGAIN WITH BOOK

FEEL MORE CONFIDENT?

NO / YES

DO PAPER AGAIN
(concentrating on your errors and questions you didn't finish)

PROCEED TO NEXT LESSON

Test Paper 1

▶ **1.2** p.9 7 MARKS

1 open   closed
Read the question! Make sure you do opposites.

2 on   off
Don't be put off by words such as 'off' which are repeated.

3 throw   catch
Make sure you do opposites, not similars.

4 false   genuine
face/mask is a compound put in here to confuse.

5 many   few
Make sure you find the most appropriate.

6 give   take
Beware of takes; take is the true opposite.

7 expensive   cheap
Beware of words such as dear which have two meanings.

▶ **1.3** p.10 7 MARKS

8 pillow/cushion
These two objects are the only ones with the same function.

9 dagger/knife
lock/key are associated but are not similar.

10 question/query
answer/explain are similar but remember it's <u>most similar</u> you're looking for.

11 calm/tranquil
thunder/lightning and stormy/waves are associated but not true similars.

12 sty/piggery
All are similar but sty/piggery is most similar.

13 dog/hound
These are most similar.

14 level/even
Read the question carefully. Odd/even is opposite.

1.5 p.12 7 MARKS

15 March   May
These are months; you may be helped by the fact they've also got capitals.

16 drink   throat
These two are associated with the others, but are different.

17 bear   dog
These two are not reptiles.

18 cheer   clap
These two express delight, the other three express pain.

19 right   left
Right and wrong are next to each other to confuse.

20 rushes   duck

21 yellow   green

1.6 p.13 12 MARKS

22–33

TRANSPORT	FABRICS	ITEMS
bicycle	wool	peg
helicopter	cotton	basket
tram	polyester	spoon
	linen	crayon
	rayon	

Look out for words that are spelt similarly but have different meanings: crayon/rayon. If you don't know where a word goes you need to make a sensible guess.

1.7 p.14 7 MARKS

34 lampshade
Don't be put off by repeated words: lamp/lamp.

35 cartwheel
There is a word 'portable' but it is spelt with one 't' and is made from the word port with the suffix able.

36 mankind
fellow and boy are connected to kind, but only man fits.

37 wardrobe
Watch out for similar words such as ward/word.

38 fireguard
There are lots of associations and links in this set but only fireguard works.

39 oneself
himself is also a compound pronoun but you must find the answer from each set of words. And watch out for homophones.

40 redhead
Watch out for homophones.

1.4 p.11 7 MARKS

41 blunt   **42** young

43 scruffy   **44** slow

45 cool   **46** soft

47 sad
With these, make sure you read the question carefully – you're looking for opposites. Make sure you're rhyming with the right word. The rhyme may rely largely on sound, so be prepared to change several letters.

1.2 p.9 7 MARKS

48 similar   alike
This is really confusing – make sure you're looking for words that are similar (such as similar/alike!)

49 warm   tepid
cold/tepid are close (tepid means 'not very warm'), but the answer given is closer.

50 brilliant   shiny
It's easy to get confused about brilliant, because it also means clever as well as bright – and the other words in the first group have been put there to confuse you.

51 pursue   chase
Read carefully: pursue and peruse look similar.

52 climb   ascend
steep/sloping are close but the words in the answer are _most_ similar.

53 slip   mistake
slip has two meanings. Again the other words in the first group are designed to put you off the trail.

54 rabbit   hare
Spelling and careful reading are essential here. Did you choose hair?

1.8 pp.14–15 7 MARKS

Read the words carefully. It's worth trying out some short words that often crop up in compound words such as by, for, on, some.

55 frog__   **56** water__

57 flash__   **58** __board

59 on__   **60** __light

61 some__ _or_ any__

► **1.1** p.8   7 MARKS

62 presents   gifts
birthday/celebration are close – but not as close
as the answer given.

63 ocean   sea
snow, ice and glacier are frozen forms of water.

64 sensible   reliable
Make sure you don't write sensible/senseless,
which are opposites.

65 creature   animal
The other three are all plant forms.

66 spin   twirl
These are all motions. Read carefully to work out
the most similar ones.

67 linger   loiter

68 monarch   ruler
rubber has been put in to confuse you about
ruler, which of course has two meanings.

► **1.4** p.11   7 MARKS

69 keen   **70** thaw
71 lazy   **72** curve
73 glossy   **74** cease
75 slender
With these, make sure you read the question
carefully – you're looking for similars. Make sure
you're rhyming with the right word. The rhyme
may rely largely on sound, so be prepared to
change several letters.

► **1.1** p.8   5 MARKS

76 Summer   Winter
None of the others are true opposites.

77 kind   unkind
caring/unkind are almost opposites, but the given
answer is closer.

78 right   wrong
Did you choose the right word? This is really a
spelling test of write, rite and right!

79 present   absent
There are several associated words here, but
only one right answer.

80 interior   exterior
This needs really careful reading. External isn't
correct: it's correct opposite would be internal.

TOTAL = 80 marks

Test Paper 2

► **2.4** pp.21–22   10 MARKS

1 span, spare, spin, spoon, spun
Here you're ordering by third letter, as they all
start sp.

2 mansion, house, flat, hut

3 warm, tepid, cold, colder, coldest
Here you're ordering by degree of coldness.

4 frog, froglet, tadpole, spawn

5 great-grandmother, grandmother, mother,
daughter, grand-daughter
Here you are ordering by age.

6 0.71, 7.01, 7.1, 71, 710
The middle one is 7.1

7 0.005, 0.09, 0.7, 1.6, 13.3
The second smallest is 0.09

8 Hugh

9 piglet

10 hippo
With questions 2, 4, 6 and 7 check for the
largest or smallest first. Make sure you've done
them the right way round. For questions 8 to 10,
write the list out in correct order on the edge of
your paper – that way you're less likely to make
a mistake.

► **1.5** p.12   5 MARKS

11 swimming   waterpolo
These two both take place in water.

12 stallion   cockerel
These two are both male.

13 cone   cuboid
These are 3D shapes, the others are 2D shapes.

14 pilot   driver
These two steer transport vehicles, the others
are transport vehicles.

15 Wales   England
The others are cities.

► **1.7** p.14   5 MARKS

16 buttercup
Cheese and milk are put in to confuse part of
the real answer: butter.

17 landmark
The others are put in to confuse you.

18 pitfall
Cave is put in to confuse part of the real answer:
pit.

19 shipwreck
The others are put in to confuse you.

20 eyesight
The others are put in to confuse you.

▶ **2.2** p.20 10 MARKS

21 ARE		**22** CAR	
23 BIT		**24** LOW	
25 END		**26** MAN	
27 RED		**28** RUG	
29 RAT		**30** BAN	

There's no foolproof way to get these.
Remember you're looking for a three-letter word.
The top tip is <u>use the sentence clue</u>.

▶ **1.8** p.14 5 MARKS

31 break__	**32** wheat__
33 bed__	**34** where__
35 air__	

Quickfire trial and error is the best method here.
If you made mistakes, read the answers carefully
and fit them with each of the words. Practice
helps with this sort of question, but in a test you
do not have time to spend too long on this. Many
of these answers you just 'see' after a while.

▶ **1.6** p.13 10 MARKS

36–45	FISH	BUILDINGS	TRANSPORT
	salmon	dovecot	jet-ski
	carp	stable	car
	pike	bike shed	pram
	minnow		

This should be ten easy marks. Look and see
where you went wrong. Possibly you didn't
recognise one of the words.

▶ **2.3** pp.20–21 10 MARKS

46 slay	**47** hope
48 them	**49** term
50 mean *or* oust	**51** beds
52 rear	**53** tone
54 shot	**55** echo

Familiarity helps with this type. You should be
able to get these right by starting on the left and
working through as explained on p. 21. However,
this can sometimes be rather lengthy. A quick
scan may save you time – sometimes the answer
will just jump out at you.

▶ **1.2** p.9 5 MARKS

56 white   black
These are the only colours which are real
opposites.

57 special   ordinary

58 float   sink
These are the most opposite.

59 down   up
This one's pretty easy!

60 day   night
Fairly easy if you work carefully.

Beware of similarities throughout this group.
Remember you're looking for opposites.

▶ **1.4** p.11 5 MARKS

61 work	**62** fast
63 hollow	**64** sunny
65 stinking	

Trial and error is necessary with these. You don't
have to do them in order if you find some easier
than others. Watch out for words that rhyme but
aren't spelled the same (lurk/work, money/sunny).

▶ **2.1** p.19 10 MARKS

66 start	**67** charge
68 soil	**69** mount
70 sage	**71** mean
72 spot	**73** kind
74 train	**75** temper

The brackets will usually contain words that will
go with one of the pairs on the left. Remember
the answer has to go with <u>both</u>. You may have
gone wrong because you didn't know the word,
in which case use a dictionary to help while
practising.

▶ **1.1** p.8 5 MARKS

76 slide   skate
Don't be confused by similar-<u>sounding</u> words:
skate, slate.

77 shimmer   shine
Same here, lots of similar-sounding words have
been put in to make your life harder!

78 peel   skin
Skin has two meanings of course. Other words
about the body have been put in to confuse.

79 bare .... naked
Remember it's most <u>similar</u>. There are some clear opposites here!

80 excursion .... trip
Careful reading here – three words with 'ex' in them are intended to make life harder!

TOTAL = 80 MARKS

Test Paper 3

▶ **3.1** p.27 10 MARKS

1 What time is supper tonight?

2 The little rabbit scampered through the long grass.

3 Pick up your pen and write this sentence.

4 The ship sank without trace.

5 She knocked at the door and entered.

6 Tom and I played in the muddy puddle.

7 Eat up your cabbage and you may have an ice cream.

8 King John was forced to sign the Magna Carta.

9 May I have a second helping please?

10 She wishes she had an elephant.
Look for clues to help you, such as question marks (question 1), proper nouns (questions 6 and 8), and words such as the and a.

▶ **3.3** p.29 10 MARKS

11 Friday   **12** knife

13 pillow   **14** owl

15 raised   **16** Pacific

17 hubbub   **18** saline

19 rye   **20** necklace
Watch out for words that seem 'right' at first glance. Did you know the meaning of all the words? If not, were you able to make a sensible guess?

▶ **3.4** p.30 10 MARKS

21-24

C	A	V	E
A			A
G	A	N	G
E			L
D	A	R	E

25-26

B	A	T
U		O
N	I	P

27-30

S	P	A	T
A			E
B	O	A	R
R			S
E	D	G	E

Read the words carefully, particularly the first and last letters. These should be fairly easy to get marks on. Try and work out why you made any mistakes.

▶ **1.4** p.11 5 MARKS

31 eat   **32** river

33 road   **34** minute

35 lake
Trial and error is necessary with these. You don't have to do them in order if you find some easier than others. Watch out for words that rhyme but aren't spelled the same: code/road.

▶ **3.2** p.28 10 MARKS

36 Please <u>come</u> to my <u>party</u> on <u>Saturday</u>.

37 13 – 3 = 10

38 James scored a <u>goal</u> in the first <u>match</u> of the <u>season</u>.

39 <u>Why</u> <u>are</u> <u>butterflies</u> so brightly coloured?

40 9 x 8 = 72

41 2 x 2 x 2

42 When mixed together, <u>yellow</u> and <u>blue</u> make <u>green</u>.

43 Please <u>wipe</u> the mud off your <u>shoes</u> on the <u>doormat</u>.

44 Simon has three <u>spoonfuls</u> of <u>sugar</u> in his <u>tea</u>.

45 I saw a <u>car</u> speeding down the <u>motorway</u> being chased by the <u>police</u>.
Follow the Megatips with these. Read carefully and work from left to right. Work methodically. Cross off any words/numbers that are definitely not right as you go along. Look in the sentence for clues, such as the verb, which make some alternatives nonsense.

2.1 p.19 5 MARKS

46 end **47** lie
48 state **49** trail
50 lame
Did you know the meaning of all the words? Were you able to make a sensible guess?

2.2 p.20 10 MARKS

51 ANT **52** VAN
53 LAP **54** TEN
55 BUT **56** RIB
57 EAT **58** CAR
59 OUT **60** MAN
There's no foolproof way to get these. Remember you're looking for a three-letter word. The top tip is use the sentence clue.

1.8 pp.14–15 5 MARKS

61 sea__ **62** battle__
63 __berry **64** bird__
65 fire__
Read the words carefully. It's worth trying out some short words that often crop up in compound words such as by, for, on, some. Certain words crop up again and again in this kind of question.

2.3 pp.20–21 10 MARKS

66 seat **67** sand
68 sour **69** whip
70 ride **71** snow
72 herd **73** mask
74 stun **75** knot
Work from the left on these and use the method outlined on page 21. Remember that a four-letter word spread across two words can be broken in three places: 1-3, 2-2, 3-1.

2.4 p.21 5 MARKS

76 calm cane care case cast
Here you're ordering by third letter, as they all start ca.

77 take tale tang tarn task
Third letter here too!

78 114 11.4 1.14 0.114
Be careful with the decimal points.

79 100kg. 1kg. 100g. 10g. 1g.
Be careful with kg and g!

80 Chloe Amy Sue Lata Penny
Did you put the youngest first?

TOTAL = 80 MARKS

Test Paper 4

4.4 p.38 5 MARKS

1 rift **2** scope
3 cinder **4** croon
5 stun
Make sure you read the question properly: 'words that can be made from the long word'. Did you cross out the letters in the short words as you checked them against the long word?

4.3 p.37 10 MARKS

6 giraffe **7** battery
8 snake **9** quintet
10 picture **11** mobile
12 ladders **13** submarine
14 quietly **15** guzzle
It's nearly always the sentence clue that will help you get these. So Megatip 1: read the question carefully! If you can't see the answer very quickly in a timed test, leave it and come back to it later. Then try juggling the letters around into combinations to see if you can get the answer that way.

4.1 p.36 10 MARKS

16 E **17** F
18 T **19** M *or* P
20 T **21** G
22 A **23** R
24 S **25** N
Look carefully at the structure of the word to do these. Experiment with different consonant blends – and be prepared for surprise vowels too, as in question 22.

▶ **3.3** p.29 5 MARKS

26	mine	**27**	kitten
28	fix	**29**	similar
30	upright		

These questions are full of red herrings – words put in to confuse you, for example in the first one: (mine yours hers). So it's really important to read carefully.

▶ **4.5** p.39 10 MARKS

31	slope	poles
32	march	charm
33	table	bleat
34	pines	snipe
35	grape	pager
36	brush	shrub
37	limes	smile
38	clasp	scalp
39	slate	stale
40	beard	bread

Read very carefully. Cross out any that are definitely <u>not</u> similar.

▶ **2.2** p.20 5 MARKS

41	TART	**42**	ABLE
43	LIMB	**44**	SENT
45	PANT		

Make sure you were looking for a <u>four</u>-letter word not a three-letter one – the number of letters can vary! These are largely questions you either 'get' or don't. So if you can't see the answer quickly, it's best to mark them and return to them at the end of the paper.

▶ **3.4** p.30 10 MARKS

46–47

P	A	T
I		A
P	A	N

or

P	I	P
A		A
T	A	N

48–51

S	I	N	G
I			L
G	A	L	A
H			D
T	O	T	E

52–55

F	I	R	E
L			V
A	C	R	E
M			R
E	N	V	Y

The key to solving these is to look at the beginning and the ends of words – look for words that start the same: fire/flame; or end the same: every/envy. This speeds up the process.

▶ **4.4** p.38 5 MARKS

56	apple	**57**	nearest
58	stack	**59**	trust
60	saviour		

Make sure you read the question carefully: words that <u>cannot</u> be made from the long word. You can cross out the letters in the short words as you go if you like – though once you've got the hang of these it's quicker not to. Don't worry if you don't know the meaning of some of these words – it's not important here.

▶ **4.2** pp.36–37 10 MARKS

61	Y	**62**	K
63	F	**64**	E
65	A	**66**	M
67	H	**68**	R
69	W	**70**	M

Look at the structure of the words and experiment. If you read carefully, the answer will very often jump out at you. Make sure the letter you choose fits both sets.

▶ **1.2** p.9 5 MARKS

71	pudding	dessert
72	pan	pot
73	combine	join
74	too	also
75	drizzle	rain

If you got some of these wrong, it may be because you chose a word that seemed similar but wasn't the <u>most</u> similar. You need to check all the options, even if the first one seems to fit: does one of the others fit even better?

▶ **2.3** pp.20–21 5 MARKS

76 twin **77** chin

78 army **79** lamb

80 veil

Read carefully, work from left to right and you should be all right here. You can follow the strategy outlined on page 21 if you need to. Sometimes you can just 'see' the answer straight away.

TOTAL = 80 MARKS

Test Paper 5

▶ **5.7** p.47 5 MARKS

1 fight **2** plane

3 trick **4** foot

5 wheat

Read carefully and follow the pattern exactly and you should be OK with these. Always ask yourself: what changed in the two words of the first pair?

▶ **5.6** pp.46–47 5 MARKS

6 eat tone

7 tie mice

8 kin glitter

9 spit care *or* site carp

10 gilt could

You can try moving one letter at a time from the first to the second words if you can't see the answer quickly.

▶ **5.1** p.43 5 MARKS

11 want **12** cloud

13 bread **14** plant

15 twin

Remember the missing letter can come anywhere in the word, not just at the end. Study the clues carefully and then experiment with the words.

▶ **3.1** p.27 5 MARKS

16 Is it time for lunch yet?

17 The dog growled at the postman.

18 My mother loves pink flowers best.

19 The museum curator asked the children to behave.

20 Sir Lancelot was one of the Knights of the Round Table.

If you had trouble with these, remember the strategies on page 27: if it has a question there will be a verb at the front; use of proper nouns as clues; clues that relate to common sense (the postman is unlikely to growl at the dog!).

▶ **4.3** p.37 10 MARKS

21 butter **22** mechanic

23 crocodile **24** liquid

25 freezing **26** towel

27 horizon **28** hospital

29 marmalade **30** butcher

Getting these will depend on one of two approaches: some have sentence clues (questions 22, 23, 24 and 30); with others you'll need to practise arranging the letters in different combinations (questions 21, 25, 26, 27, 28 and 29).

▶ **3.2** pp.28–29 10 MARKS

31	28	4	6
32	5	x	125
33	camouflage	owl	branch
34	Brushing	teeth	them
35	33	–	15
36	fell	her	kitchen
37	time	go	bed
38	Sixty	33	27
39	eat	your	vegetables
40	36	6	6

You need to work carefully and methodically using the method outlined on pages 28–29. Cross out the obviously wrong words as you go along.

▶ **4.1** p.36 10 MARKS

41 E **42** T

43 K **44** P

45 S **46** F

47 M *or* Y **48** E *or* O

49 W **50** D *or* M

If you were stuck at any point, try running through the alphabet letter by letter to check possibilities. Look out for vowels (as in questions 41 and 48), since they can be harder to spot.

▶ **5.2** p.44 5 MARKS

51 ride   **52** right

53 trip   **54** price

55 stale

    If you can't see these straight away from the clue, try taking away one letter at a time.

▶ **2.4** pp.21–22 5 MARKS

56 laid   maid   paid   raid   said

57 spade   speck   spike   sponge   sport

58 sweet wrapper   A4 paper   newspaper skyscraper

59 matchbox   shoebox   hatbox   horse box

60 sand grain   pebble   brick concrete block

    Take care with alphabetical order. Use common sense on questions 58 to 60.

▶ **5.8** pp.48–49 10 MARKS

61 THAN

    Third and fourth letters of first word, first and fourth of second word.

62 LEAF

    Third and fourth letters of second word, third of first word, first of first word.

63 OPEN

    Third and first letters of first word, first and second letters of second word.

64 PORE

    Third letter of first word, second letter of second word, first and fourth of first word.

65 LEAD

    Second, third and fourth letter of second word, first letter of first word.

66 GARB

    Fourth, third, second and first of first word.

67 FELT

    Second and third of first word (reversed), then first and fourth of second word.

68 STEP

    Third and fourth letters (reversed), then first and second (reversed) from first word.

69 NICK

    Third of first word, third of second word, first of second word, fourth of first word.

70 TENT

    Second and third of first word, then first and third of second word.

If you have difficulty doing these, try drawing arrows from the two outside words to the middle word of the left hand set to get the pattern – as on pages 48–49. You will find that in some of these, the middle word could get a letter from more than one place. You then have to see which option works with the second set.

▶ **5.4** p.45 5 MARKS

71 SLOT

    P and T have to change. You have to try each option. SPOW is not a word, SLOW is.

72 CLAN

    C and W have to change.

73 PEEL

    Care needs to be taken with spelling; PEEL is a word, FEAL is not.

74 LACE

    Change the F to an L.

75 CONE

    Change the first N to a C.

▶ **5.3** p.44 5 MARKS

76 b   **77** c

78 a   **79** d

80 g

    If you can't 'see' these quickly, you can use trial and error working through the alphabet.

TOTAL = 80 MARKS

Test Paper 6

▶ **6.2** p.55 5 MARKS

1 26 27

    These go forward in ones.

2 61 66

    These go forward in fives and the corresponding number in each pair increases by 6.

3 040

    These go forward in tens and the corresponding number in each pair increases by 3.

4 56 58

    These go forward in twos.

5 26 20

    These go back in sixes and the corresponding number in each pair decreases by 7.

6.3 p.55 5 MARKS

6 35f
Numbers forward in sevens, letters forward in ones.

7 s3t
Both sets of letters go forward in twos, numbers back in ones.

8 12r
Numbers back in twos, letters back in ones.

9 28S32
Both sets of numbers forward in eights, letters back in ones.

10 T24S
Both sets of letters back in twos, numbers back in eights.

4.2 pp.36–37 10 MARKS

11 N		**12** D	
13 P		**14** T	
15 Y		**16** M	
17 B		**18** H	
19 K		**20** L	

Work through the alphabet letter by letter if you can't quickly 'see' these.

5.4 p.45 5 MARKS

21 HONK	**22** DAZE
23 BROW	**24** LENT
25 HOOF	

Remember to write in the letters which don't change first. This makes it easier to test which is the correct letter that changes in the middle word.

6.1 p.54 5 MARKS

26 P Q
Letters move forward two.

27 K M
Letters move forward three.

28 V U
Letters move back two.

29 R V
Letters move forward five.

30 N K
Letters move back five.

6.4 p.56 10 MARKS

31 hand   **32** four

33 foot   **34** nephew

35 green   **36** dry

37 sunset   sunrise

38 football boots   golf shoes

39 Rook   diamonds

40 bread   cement

There's no easy way to get these. You just have to read carefully and find the answer that fits best.

5.2 p.44 5 MARKS

41 SEND	**42** CASE
43 CONE	**44** MEAT
45 TICKET	

If you can't 'see' these easily, trying crossing out one letter at a time.

4.4 p.38 5 MARKS

46 crease	**47** about
48 crust	**49** crate
50 cease	

Look particularly for repeat letters and extra vowels.

5.7 p.47 5 MARKS

51 well	**52** hook
53 shadier	**54** matter
55 cheat	

You will need to study the first pair carefully to see what changes, then apply it to the second word.

4.5 p.39 5 MARKS

56 table	bleat
57 petal	pleat
58 stool	tools
59 sheet	these
60 parted	depart

Work through methodically left to right. Check the first word on the left against all the others, then the second, then the third, and so on.

6.5 pp.57–58 5 MARKS

61 JL   VX

Gaps of one letter between each letter in a pair and between each pair of letters.

62 ZY   WV
Letter order reversed and gaps of one letter between each pair.

63 Gi   Km
Gaps of one letter between each capital letter and between each lower case letter.

64 IL   QT
Gaps of two letters between each letter in a pair, and in sequence between each pair.

65 DW   EV
The first letter in each pair goes forward one starting from A, the second letter in each pair moves back one starting from Z.

▶ **6.7** pp.59–60   5 MARKS

66 10Z   20U
Numbers move forward two, letters back one.

67 F29   H26
Letters move forward two, numbers back three.

68 39e   43g
Numbers forward four, letters forward two.

69 ef12   qr18
Letter pairs move forward two, numbers forward two.

70 a12Z   b10Y
Lower case letters forward one, numbers back two, capital letters back one.

▶ **5.3** p.44   5 MARKS

71 s   **72** t
73 b   **74** g
75 c
Experiment with different letters if you can't 'see' these.

▶ **6.6** pp.58–59   5 MARKS

76 20   30
Forward five.

77 31   23
Back four.

78 24   96
Double each number.

79 6   4
The sequence is –10, –8, –6, –4, –2.

80 36   30
Back six (it's easier to work from the right-hand end here).

TOTAL = 80 MARKS

Test Paper 7

▶ **7.1** p.64   5 MARKS

1 g   **2** j
3 f   **4** j
5 g
Always write the values down before you do the calculation. You're less likely to make a slip that way. Remember two letters without a sign means multiply.

▶ **5.8** pp.48–49   5 MARKS

6 RATE
First two letters of last word then middle two letters of first word, reversed.

7 FELT
First letter of first word, then middle two letters of last word, then third letter of first word.

8 NEED
Last letter of first word, second of last word, third of first word, first of last word.

9 TAKE
Fourth and second of first word, then first and second of last word.

10 VASE
First letter of first word, middle two letters of last word, then first letter of last word.

▶ **7.1** p.64   5 MARKS

11 12   **12** 12
13 11   **14** 15
15 9
Always write the values down before you do the calculation. You're less likely to make a slip that way.

▶ **5.1** p.43   5 MARKS

16 brush   **17** thick
18 saucer   **19** think
20 sport
Work through the alphabet if you can't see any of these quickly.

▶ **5.2** p.44   5 MARKS

21 lush   **22** titter
23 gasp   **24** wiggle
25 gash

6.2 p.55 5 MARKS

26 9　　　　6
There is a gap of three between each pair and the corresponding numbers in each decrease by 4.

27 90　　　100
There is a gap of ten between each pair.

28 49　　　47
Each pair goes back two.

29 33　　　44
Each pair goes up 11.

30 4　　　　44
The first number in each pair goes down by one, the second down by 11.

5.6 pp.46–47 5 MARKS

31 HOT　　SOON
32 PLY　　AWAY
33 RIM　　TWIN
34 SLIT　　WARP
35 CHIP　　BROOM
You will have to experiment with removing each letter in turn from the first word if you can't quickly 'see' these.

6.4 p.56 5 MARKS

36 goose
37 breathing
38 strings
39 chuckle　　glare
40 meringues　　chocolate
Not all the questions are exactly the same. Be careful with the brackets in the last two questions.

7.2 pp.65–67 10 MARKS

41 243　　　　**42** PETS
43 4235　　　**44** 3641
45 6431　　　**46** 5163
47 DQQM　　　**48** PEN
49 CARE　　　**50** TRACE
Write down the answer as you go along. It's very easy to make a slip when turning words into code.

6.3 p.55 5 MARKS

51 16W
Numbers forward four, letters back one.

52 k12l
The alphabet is in order, the numbers go forward two.

53 20t
Numbers back ten, letters forward two.

54 WD15
The letters work in from each end of the alphabet, the numbers back five.

55 21Q24
The numbers go up in threes, letters back two.

5.5 p.46 5 MARKS

56 SORE　　BORE
57 SOOT　　SLOT
58 MIRE　　MINE
59 FOND　　FORD
60 SILL or WILT　　SILT
If you have trouble with these you'll need to study the examples on page 46 again. Always write in the letters that remain unchanged throughout first.

6.6 pp.58–59 5 MARKS

61 9　　　　15
Forward three.

62 23　　　15
Back two.

63 10　　　20
Forward ten.

64 16　　　20
Forward four.

65 56　　　28
Back seven.

7.3 pp.68–69 10 MARKS

66–67 Kong
Underline those which like bananas. Then see which of those don't eat dates.

68–69 None of the 3-bedroom houses are for sale
Be careful with this one.

70–71 Tom

72–73 clarinet

74–75 Harry

Left Column

▶ **7.3** pp.68–69 5 MARKS

76–77 They all speak at least two languages.
They all speak Russian.

78 Natasha   **79** Boris

80 Tanya

TOTAL = 80 MARKS

Test Paper 8

▶ **7.1** p.64 5 MARKS

1 e   **2** a

3 d   **4** d

5 c
Always write the values down before you do the calculation. You're less likely to make a slip that way. Remember two letters without a sign means multiply.

▶ **5.5** p.46 5 MARKS

6 SLAP   SLAB

7 CANE *or* LAVE   LANE

8 PATS   PITS

9 LIVE   LIFE

10 SLAY   SLAT *or* SPAY
If you have trouble with these you'll need to study the examples on page 46 again. Always write in the letters that remain unchanged throughout first.

▶ **3.1** p.27 5 MARKS

11 How are you feeling today?

12 Mr and Mrs Brown walked down the road holding hands.

13 My goldfish is twice the size of yours.

14 Red and blue mixed together make purple.

15 The mouse on my computer has frozen.
If you can't 'see' these quickly, you'll have to work down the line systematically, following the method on page 27.

▶ **7.1** p.64 5 MARKS

16 13   **17** 15

18 11   **19** 15

20 20

Right Column

▶ **4.4** p.38 6 MARKS

21 mini   **22** pace

23 since   **24** nets

25 train   **26** acre
Make sure you read the instructions carefully! They change half way through.

▶ **6.3** p.55 7 MARKS

27 6d
Each letter and number moves on one.

28 18V
Numbers move on two, letters move back one.

29 50z
Numbers move on five, letters move on two.

30 kL18
Each set of letters follows on directly, numbers move on three.

31 44n7
First set of numbers move back 11, letters move on one, second number moves back one.

32 dw28
The letters in each pair start at opposite ends of the alphabet and move in, the numbers go up in fours.

33 T54s
Capital letters move back one, numbers move back nine, lower case letters move on one.

▶ **7.2** pp.65–67 10 MARKS

34 TEA   **35** 7234

36 WASTE   **37** 3265

38 50235   **39** 6234

40 4065   **41** RICE

42 FIRE   **43** REEF
Write down the answer as you go along. It's very easy to make a slip when turning words into code.

▶ **2.2** p.20 5 MARKS

44 WIND   **45** WALL

47 SHED   **47** RAVE *or* AVER

48 EASE
The sentence is your best clue to doing these. Read each one through a few times to see if it gives you any clues.

▶ 6.4 p.56 10 MARKS

49 brother   **50** leg

51 goose   **52** garage *or* carport

53 France

54 light   dark

55 green   orange

56 quiver   scabbard

57 road   brook

58 coat   trousers

There's no easy way to get these. You just have to read carefully and find the answer that fits best.

▶ 7.3 pp.68–69 6 MARKS

59 6

60 4

61 male

62 male

63 trodden on (by a cow)

63 6

It's important to ignore the irrelevant information, such as the names of the parents, and to focus on the key details.

▶ 1.3 p.10 5 MARKS

65 cup/mug

66 pencil/pen

67 stone/rock

68 correct/right

69 pail/bucket

70 tepid/warm

Remember you're looking for similar; also that you're looking for the most similar – you may have an answer which you think is right, but check the others as well.

▶ 6.5/6/7 pp.57–60 10 MARKS

71 OP   UV

Each pair is separated from the next by a one-letter gap.

72 Sr   On

Both capital and lower case letters move back with one-letter gaps and all the letters are in sequence going backwards.

73 ef   ij

Each pair is separated by a two-letter gap.

74 YB   WD

The pairs start from either ends of the alphabet, going back by one letter and forward by one letter.

75 efg   fgh

Each letter in each group continues on one letter from the last one.

76 18G   27P

The numbers go up in threes. The letters go up in threes.

77 az7   cx21

The first letter in each group is one on from the previous one. The second one is one back. The numbers go up in sevens.

78 12   6

The numbers halve each time.

79 61   53

The numbers decrease by four each time.

80 2Ii   64Nn

The numbers double. Both the capital and the lower case letters move on one each time.

TOTAL = 80 MARKS

Record your score

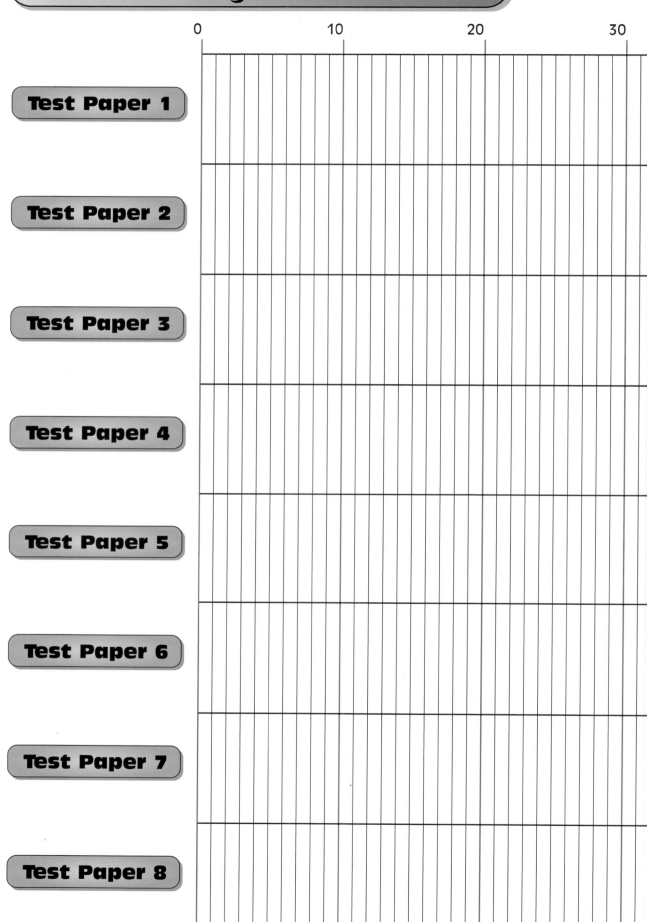

Test Paper 1

Test Paper 2

Test Paper 3

Test Paper 4

Test Paper 5

Test Paper 6

Test Paper 7

Test Paper 8